You Have Mail From God!

Second Lesson Sermons For Advent/Christmas/Epiphany Cycle C

Harold C. Warlick, Jr.

CSS Publishing Company, Inc., Lima, Ohio

YOU HAVE MAIL FROM GOD!

Copyright © 2000 by
CSS Publishing Company, Inc.
Lima, Ohio

All rights reserved. No part of this publication may be reproduced in any manner whatsoever without the prior permission of the publisher, except in the case of brief quotations embodied in critical articles and reviews. Inquiries should be addressed to: Permissions, CSS Publishing Company, Inc., P.O. Box 4503, Lima, Ohio 45802-4503.

From the *Holy Bible, New International Version,* Copyright © 1973, 1978, 1984 International Bible Society. Used by permission of Zondervan Bible Publishers. All rights reserved.

Library of Congress Cataloging-in-Publication Data

Warlick, Harold C.
    You have mail from God! : second lesson sermons for Advent/Christmas/Epiphany, Cycle C / Harold C. Warlick, Jr.
      p. cm.
    Includes bibliographical references.
    ISBN 0-7880-1743-8 (alk. paper)
      1. Advent sermons. 2. Christmas sermons. 3. Epiphany season—Sermons. 4. Bible. O.T. Gospels—Sermons. 5. Sermons, American. I. Title.
BV4254.5 W38 2000
252'.61—dc21   00-035803
                                                                                                                         CIP

This book is available in the following formats, listed by ISBN:
    0-7880-1743-8   Book
    0-7880-1744-6   Disk
    0-7880-1745-4   Sermon Prep

For more information about CSS Publishing Company resources, visit our website at www.csspub.com.

PRINTED IN U.S.A.

*Dedicated to David Humphreys
and M. B. Morrow,
in appreciation for decades
of wise counsel and heightened
friendship*

Table Of Contents

Introduction	7
Advent 1 The Future Shapes The Present 1 Thessalonians 3:9-13	11
Advent 2 Divide And Destroy Philippians 1:3-11	17
Advent 3 Truce Or Peace? Philippians 4:4-7	23
Advent 4 Role Reversal: Baby And Priest Hebrews 10:5-10	29
Christmas Eve/Day Having To Stay When You Want Out Titus 2:11-14	33
Christmas 1 The Next Step Colossians 3:12-17	37
Christmas 2 A Secret Is Finally Revealed Ephesians 1:3-14	43
Ephiphany From Crumbs To Half A Loaf Ephesians 3:1-12	51

Epiphany 1   55
(Baptism Of Our Lord)
    The Scattering Of Lesser Figures
    Acts 8:14-17

Epiphany 2   61
    What Are Spiritual Gifts For?
    1 Corinthians 12:1-11

Epiphany 3   67
    Respect
    1 Corinthians 12:12-31a

Epiphany 4   73
    Old Favorite
    1 Corinthians 13:1-13

Epiphany 5   79
    Good News For Good Living
    1 Corinthians 15:1-11

Epiphany 6   85
    A Note To Fearful Hearts
    1 Corinthians 15:12-20

Epiphany 7   89
    The Power Of Uninformed Decisions
    1 Corinthians 15:35-38, 42-50

Epiphany 8   95
    Taking The Sting Out Of Death
    1 Corinthians 15:51-58

Transfiguration Of Our Lord   101
(Last Sunday After The Epiphany)
    Exposed!
    2 Corinthians 3:12 — 4:2

Introduction

The decision to tackle the epistle lessons for Advent, Christmas, and Epiphany was no small one. Advent is the name we give to the season of "expectation" which lies before the birth of our Lord. Epiphany is the term we employ in the Western tradition to speak of the season when we remember the "showing forth" of Christ to the Gentiles. What better assignment than to labor with the "expectation" that in a season habitually buried under selected Old Testament prophecies and Gospel beauty spots, the one named Paul, who bridged in personhood and theology these sometimes disparate worlds of prophecy and gospel thereby creating the ministry to us Gentiles, will actually get a hearing (and a preaching)? Paul's letters, both the authentic and attributed ones, are lasting attempts to show forth Christ to us Gentiles. It is the contention of this author that his words, if rightly examined and appropriated, are as relevant to struggling Christians today as when they were originally penned and read.

At the very least, it is hoped that these messages will provide preachers with more than throw-ins from Paul as they forage for material among the Old Testament and Gospel lessons.

Obviously the messages assert that the texts about Paul and attributed to Paul possess transhistorical value. When certain portions of the texts are historically conditioned, the author has tried to acknowledge that fact. On the whole, however, the following messages have sought to affirm the relevance and criticality of the defining characteristics of the Pauline messages without attempting to criticize, tear apart, and otherwise totally deconstruct Paul's efforts to address complex issues with a measure of certitude. Underlying Paul's theology is his constant admission that while Christ crucified appeared impotent and foolish to the world, Christ crucified was the power and wisdom of God in action for the church.

While some may view preaching from the epistle lessons during this season as, indeed, a fallible and foolish exercise, it is hoped that in some small way these messages will enable the reader to realize that these texts are full of God's hidden redemptive power.

Many of us at various times in our lives have bowed our heads to both true and false images of Paul. Some have even contended that Paul was the inventor of a new religion, totally unlike the religion taught by Jesus. Others have used pseudo-Pauline passages to justify everything from slavery to oppression of females and minorities. Whether viewed as a myth maker, unregenerated Pharisee, or vital champion of freedom, Paul is one whose writings demand our attention. Certainly the study of Paul's theology will remain a formidable challenge for even the best of preachers.

Paul's letters came from one who daily had to deal with the practical struggles of running a newly created organization. Consequently he is a valuable resource for today's minister who is trying to maintain a Christian community in an interconnected and spiritually struggling world. Advent, Christmas, and Epiphany are not times to drop Paul from sermons or try to domesticate him to fit preconceived notions about church programs.

Paul's persuasive efforts to structure, organize, and keep alive communities of followers of Jesus commend themselves to us. Just as the birth of Jesus was a time bomb that later exploded and split time between B.C. and A.D., Paul's letters seem to have served that function for the church throughout its plodding history. Martin Luther read Paul and began a Reformation of dramatic political and social consequences. Feminist theologians read Paul and utilized his freedom from the law arguments to embrace utopian visions of the eschatological community where there would be "neither Greek nor Jew, neither male nor female, neither slave nor free."

Even the present season beckons us to utilize the methods of Paul. Christmas itself is celebrated on December 25, a day tied to the pagan feast of the winter solstice. Our season is an example of creative Christian thinking which blended together the secular respect for a season with the sacredness of a religious observance. In a day when American churches are badly frightened by social change and are clinging to their separate identities come what may, perhaps the missionary who embraced change and blended together "under the shadow of Jesus" a profound message of freedom that liberated Christian churches from their captivity to a confining heritage can liberate our churches as well.

All published sermons invite literary and exegetical judgments. The author hopes the sermons in this volume will prove to be acceptable.

Thanks are due to Shirley Connor, who typed the manuscript, and Dean Vance Davis, whose definition of professional growth and faculty development expands annually to include sermon development. Chuck Hutchens, Bob Ferguson, and Bob Williams, colleagues in the ministry, offered helpful comments and words of encouragement.

Best wishes as you strive for new depths of simplicity and insight to illuminate God's nature and activity through your preaching.

Harold C. Warlick, Jr.
High Point, North Carolina

Advent 1

The Future Shapes The Present

1 Thessalonians 3:9-13

Sometimes you and I read the Bible as if it were a blast from the past. In reality, it also sends us future messages about what it means for each of us to be a child of God and a disciple of Jesus Christ. Scripture is often out ahead of us, inviting us to live a richer and nobler life today. In essence, today's epistle lesson is a fax from tomorrow concerning how Christians are to respond to the great promise of God's return or reappearance before humankind.

A necessary piece of equipment for many modern offices is a fax machine. A business person conveyed an interesting experience he had with a fax machine. Some friends of his in Australia sent him a fax. As he read it, he noticed the date the fax was transmitted. It was sent and dated tomorrow. The fax was sent to him the day after he had received it because of Australia's time zone. He labeled the letter his "fax from the future."[1]

Fittingly, the first Sunday of Advent is symbolized by lighting the candle of Promise. As the days shorten and the nights deepen, we know of darkness. Like the early Thessalonians we are anxious and lacking in our faith. Yet we light a candle as a sign of God's promise that the Light of the Christ has come and will come again. That promise shapes our present.

Today's lesson comes from one of the very few letters from Paul that does not try to combat a particular problem in the early church. Paul's words are those of one who misses his new converts who have no tradition to fall back on in his absence. Like all new converts, they have to fall forward into the future to articulate who they are.

Consequently, Paul writes to reassure them in the midst of their anxiety and answer some questions about the promise of the day of the Lord.

Sometimes we hear the adage, "the present shapes the future." Indeed it does. We live in a world of cause and effect, rewards and punishments, and impulses and impressions. Paul points to another reality. It is just as true for humankind that the future shapes the present.

Over the entrance to Andover Hall at Harvard Divinity school is an inscription in Latin which translates into English, "The end is determined by the beginning." Were Paul to have charge of that emblem, the verbiage would, perhaps, be reversed, "The beginning is determined by the end."

Apparently the hearers of this epistle in Thessalonica were filled with speculation and anxiety about the day when the Lord would return. Would it really happen? Would it be in our lifetime? How do we live in the present? Is God any more available in the future than God is available now? What is the basis for our hope?

The country philosopher contends that the Bible pictures life as it never was, so we can see life as it really is. Paul attempts to ground the newly born Christians of Thessalonica in the vision of a promise that the Jesus who came once in weakness and in meekness will come again, "with all his holy ones," so they can live in love toward one another and everyone else, confident of God's future.

Peter Gomes has noted that the glorious paradox of Advent is that "as we look forward to the return of the past, the rekindling of the lights that lead to Bethlehem, we look forward also to that which has not yet been, the lights that lead to the eternal victory we shall share in Jesus Christ."[2] Indeed, Advent, if not the entire Christian experience, is seeing life as it never was so we can see life as it really is.

Without the vision of a future which can shape our present, Advent ceases to become a transforming event. It becomes a spot on the calendar, the four Sundays which precede Christmas. When Prince Talleyrand, the great French statesman, was an old man, he attended a large ball given on some diplomatic occasion. At one point in the evening an announcement was brought to the assembled crowd. The messenger read a statement that Napoleon Bonaparte had died. In the silence that followed, the guests looked to Talleyrand for some words. He simply said, "*It is no longer an event. It is merely a piece of information.*"[3] Something akin to this experience happens when people gather in modern day cathedrals and churches to pay homage to a former faith that now pales in the midst of a long played-out commercial scene of candles, readings, carols, and gifts. No longer an event, merely a piece of information — Advent begins today!

It seems somewhat consistent in human history that without a transforming confidence in God's future, what Christians call "eschatology," yesterday's big events become today's "mere pieces of information." We are able to find joy, even in our present darkness, precisely because we believe in the promise of a coming dawn in which the weaknesses and tribulations of this world can be seen for what they really are and are not!

This ability of the future to shape the present connects us intimately and eternally with the anxious Thessalonians. Let's be honest. Are not their questions our questions as we approach this Christmas season? Reflect on what lies ahead of us. We will sing of peace in the world as we belt out those familiar Christmas carols. Joy to the World — "He rules the world with peace and grace, and makes the nations prove the glories of his righteousness and wonders of his love." Hark! The Herald Angels Sing — "Peace on earth and mercy mild, God and sinners reconciled!" Silent Night — "Holy infant so tender and mild, sleep in heavenly peace, sleep in heavenly peace."

Why do we keep singing those songs? Why do we keep singing those songs, if it appears that peace is hardly winning? Certainly all is neither calm nor bright in the annals of human history. In our last 100 years over 125 million people have died in wars. Many children wake up Christmas morning in rooms with parents who have abused them in the previous year. Why do we keep singing those songs of peace every year? Is our big event just a foregone piece of information to a weary world?

When I was a teenager there was a high school in our area that lost all its football games three years in a row. They never won a single game. Every time we went on the field and bowled them over, I was amazed at the surroundings. They had a large band that played over and over, "Fight to win the victory, fight for her name." And all those parents and students would stand up and sing. They always had a dozen or more cheerleaders brightly dressed in green and white. They'd spell out V-I-C-T-O-R-Y all through the game. I used to wonder what it was like to puff your breath out on the tuba or keep screaming "victory" in the freezing cold and rain when your team always lost. Oh, sometimes they would be ahead in the game, but at the end the idea of victory never became a reality. They always cheered for the idea but the reality never came.

Why sing and plan for an idea that never becomes a total accomplishment? Why not save everybody the time, the effort, and the money and just never take the uniforms and the instruments out of the closet? Why sing for an idea that never becomes an accomplishment?

Jesus the Christ, like the prophets before him, let forth the dream of a world of peace, where the will of God would be done, a kingdom of God where the lion would lie down with the lamb; where the king on the throne would be the Prince of Peace and not a totalitarian despot. He said his Spirit, his Holy Spirit, would be here to support it. But it doesn't seem to have happened.

To be quite honest, even in the day of Jesus there was a dark side to Christmas. There was no peace on earth. At the human level it appeared that nothing had changed. The rivers of the Middle East still ran red with blood. Within two years of the birth of Jesus, Herod was slaughtering all the male babies in Bethlehem two years old and under. People had to keep paying taxes to Rome and bowing down before the emperor. The lions in the Roman coliseum feasted on the flesh of those who had believed that Jesus was the Prince of Peace. Apparently this messiah was not just about love and light and peace. Jesus the Christ was not just about singing songs and having a warm feeling in your heart. Jesus Christ was not just about going to heaven when you die and living in a perfect world on earth until that time. Jesus Christ was about sin, judgment, and forgiveness. The very fact that Jesus was born as the Son of God was witness to the reality of human sin.

Sometimes the complexities of a tough world blind us to our sources for hope. We walk and act as if nothing has changed when everything has changed. One of the craziest acts in the Bible is attributed to Jeremiah. Jeremiah knew that God had promised peace for his people and that God had said he would give them a new covenant, not on stone tablets but on human hearts. Yet, Judah was weak and about to be swallowed up by the Chaldeans. The people of Judah had lost faith in everything. Jeremiah held to God's long-term promise. As a result of his faith and hope, Jeremiah took his life savings and purchased property, land, in Judah which he knew would be destroyed. Scripture says he paid full price for it, too. *He was more interested in buying into the promise of a kingdom of peace than being ruled by what the world could see at the present.*

This is precisely what Paul was encouraging the anxious Thessalonians to do. He was urging a most radical transformation under the shadow of Jesus' promise to return. This transformation could actually make one's love increase, not only toward one's comrades-in-arms, but toward everyone else as well.

Bastions of pessimism in our world will always look at the scriptural images of Jesus, Paul, and Jeremiah and exclaim, "Quit singing those songs of peace. There is no peace on earth and there never will be. All you religious folk are unrealistic dreamers. You can talk about peace and love, but the world ain't that way."

We stand at the threshold as surely as did those Thessalonians who first read Paul's letter. Will it really happen? Night and day we will need to have others praying for us that we may be supplied what is lacking in our faith. We so desperately want our God and our Lord Jesus to clear the way for us through our commercialism, insensitivity, and violence, so the confident message of hope in God's future can come to us.

We will sing the songs. We will light the candles. We will embrace the choirs and the ministers as they come again to cheer us through another season and supply what is lacking in our faith. We will preach of justice when there is no justice. We will talk of love when all around us there is hate. We will lift up compassion when ugliness is our ever-present reality. We will stage pageants of shepherds, stars, and wisemen, recalling, perhaps, scenes from life like it never was in order to see our life as it really is. We will do this in joy and overflowing love, not to celebrate a birthday and profane the nativity scene of a messiah, but to express our confidence in God's future. It is that future that shapes our present and turns this season back into a big event.

---

1. The story is told by Brian Kelly Bauknight in *On A Wing and A Prayer* (Nashville: Dimension for Living, 1998), p. 23.

2. Peter J. Gomes, *Sermons: Biblical Wisdom for Daily Living* (New York: William Morrow, 1998), p. 20.

3. As quoted by Herbert O. Driscoll, *Year of the Lord* (Toronto, Anglican Book Center, 1986), p. 104.

Advent 2

Divide And Destroy

Philippians 1:3-11

One day at a city gate two women were arguing over a baby. King Solomon said, "Well, first take a sword, cut the baby into two equal pieces, and give each mother a half." Of course, you could only divide the baby by destroying it.

The most vital items in our faith are like that. You can only divide them by destroying them. They are entities, not quantities. The Holy Spirit is an entity. Each part belongs to every other part. The Bible itself is an entity; it is an organic whole. In our modern mindset, hinging often on the primacy of specialization, we are tempted to affirm the expression, "Divide and Conquer." Faith wants to underscore a unity that transcends diversity, division, and specialization.

The biggest and best aspects of the Christian faith cannot be halved or divided. The good news of Jesus Christ overcomes the diversity of who we are, how we worship, our present circumstances, and what we believe in our own little groups. F. W. Boreham[1] has reminded us that our universe consists of two sets of things; there are *Quantities*, and there are *Entities*. Life in the long run revolves around its entities.

A pound of butter is a quantity; you can divide it without doing it injury. A quart of milk is a quantity; you can pour it into several glasses without in any way destroying it as good milk.

You hear a person proclaiming, "I believe in the ethical portions of the Bible. Give me those passages that make for justice and love of neighbor and integrity. Give me the Ten Commandments; give me the Sermon on the Mount; give me the prophets; give me the Golden Rule."

And another person proclaims just as loudly: "Give me the Evangelical. Give me John 3:16. Give me the story of the cross! Give me the precious promises of the New Testament."

It cannot be done. To divide the Bible is to destroy it. How does the person so insistent on the ethical aspect of Scripture remove the stain from his or her own soul without that Savior given out of God's love to the whole world? How? You can describe yourself as a feminist who contends that God is a male construct used to oppress women. Fine. But how do you understand the mystery of life and walk through the difficulties of life without a God who loved the world enough to send the Christ to guide you?

And let those who are so insistent on the evangelical ask themselves a question. Ignore the prophets, the Sermon on the Mount, the Golden Rule, and truthful perspectives like those of the feminists. To what extent will people respect *your* message? They will turn from your arrogance and naiveté with contempt.

This oneness, this living in *partnership* with the whole gospel, calls forth the ultimate in knowledge and depth of insight if one is to discern what is best. Paul's words to the Philippians emphasize that growth in Christ is *relational not mechanical* and that there is but one single gospel in whose service we are all partners.

In our day, Paul's letters do not often serve as the basis for the Sunday sermon. In the season of Advent it is especially rare to hear a sermon centered on a Pauline letter. One reason why this is the case is that many people, including preachers, possess a rather narrow perception of "the gospel." They view the gospel as divided into four quantities and share a story from one of the four canonical Gospels. Consequently the appointed passage is taken from one of these four Gospels and becomes the subject of the Sunday sermon. Certainly the good news or "joy" in Christ transcends any one of the four stories about Jesus that have been preserved from earliest times.[2]

Tradition has it that there is only a single gospel, not four. We possess four versions of an indivisible gospel. Paul shares this traditional view that there is but one single gospel. Consequently he can forcefully remind his hearer that they are in *partnership with the gospel.*

In our contemporary world of specialization, division, and quantification, no greater need looms before us in the Advent season than this sense of connectedness. Advent and Easter, darkness and light, bondage and exodus, exile and homecoming, Jew and Gentile, Shepherd and King, stable and star, baby and Messiah and, yes, prison and joy — all are one. In Paul's statement of gratitude for his relationship with the church (Philippians 1:3-11), he states in parallel phrases a twofold gratitude: his remembrance of them and their partnership in the gospel.

Commentators refer to Philippians as the "epistle of joy" and wonder why the word occurs so often, especially in a letter to close friends who are heavy with the news of Paul's being in prison and facing death.[3] Yet one must remember Paul's insistence on the gospel and life's experiences as an entity. A Thanksgiving is part of all his letters except Galatians. He is thanking God for the Phillipians' intimate partnership in the proclamation of the gospel.

Today's lesson seems especially appropriate for the Advent and Christmas season. Paul is grateful for the Philippians' generous sharing in the gospel ministry ever since he first presented them with his message. The Philippians have repeatedly shared in the spread of the gospel by financially aiding Paul (1 Thessalonians 4:16, 2 Corinthians 11:9). In many respects they are his favorite congregation. He longs for them with a view that they are in the very heart of Christ. The letter expresses great mutual affection.

Perhaps this is a message all of us need to hear at this particular time of year. Those of us who are in practical partnership with the Advent and Christmas programs of the church often work our way through the season with a love-hate mentality. While some may have a holiday card image in their minds, with chestnuts roasting on an open fire, the season often becomes a problem-solving one:
- It's the last month to raise the church budget.
- When the last Christmas Eve Communion Service candle is extinguished the minister often will sigh, "Thank God!"
- The choral director, weary from cantatas and choir parties, will slump in the recliner from exhaustion.

- The hurried, frantic shopper will sit on the floor surrounded by reams of wrapping paper and yards of ribbon.
- The calendar will be loaded with Sunday school parties and frantic visits to relatives.

To be certain, Advent and Christmas often become problems to be solved instead of a partnership to be affirmed. Chuck Hutchens, a United Methodist minister in Taylorsville, North Carolina, had a particular problem one Advent season. A Christmas season dinner party was scheduled for 6 p.m. one evening. Chuck arrived home at 5 p.m. to begin helping his wife with the housecleaning. The house looked great! The tree was beautifully decorated, the dining room table was gorgeous, the pleasant smell of scented candles filled the rooms, and the sounds of Christmas music echoed throughout the home. But at 5:10 p.m. the doorbell rang. There stood two guests who thought the Christmas dinner was at 5 p.m. And there stood the hosts in their sweat suits. *The house was ready but the hosts were not!* The external problems were solved but the progress of the hosts in getting themselves ready was abruptly cut off. One of the essential aspects for the church is the necessity of not separating the programs of Advent from preparation of the people themselves for the season.

How appropriate, then, to utilize this Scripture of thanks and joy. Ben Witherington[4] has pointed out that the letter of Philippians is more of a progress-oriented than a problem-solving letter. Though there were still things that had to be overcome in Philippi, Paul exuded confidence and expressed hope about how things would turn out for his converts and himself.

Paul's methodology of establishing positive feelings between himself and his audience speaks to us as we move through this season. It is through our love for one another that our partnership with Christ is sealed. Indeed, it is this love that enables us to discern what is best.

Have you ever wondered how people are trained to detect counterfeit money? I mean some fake money looks just like the real thing. The American Banking Association sponsors a two-week training program. The program is unique in how it helps tellers detect counterfeit bills. Not once during the two-week training does a teller ever see a single counterfeit bill. Not once do they listen to a lecture describing the characteristics of counterfeit money. All they do for two weeks is handle authentic currency. Hour after hour, and day after day they just handle the real stuff. *At the end of the training they have become so familiar with the authentic that they are never fooled by the false.* The people themselves are prepared.

Paul's words challenge us to see creation as basically good and God constantly acting in and through history. While we do not live in first century Philippi and we have never heard Saint Paul preach, we have to live out our faith in the world of our time as they did in theirs.

We move forward, handling the best, confident that the one who began the good work in us will see it through to its completion. After all, we are partners in an entity, *the* gospel of Christ, not competitors in a contest. We are not hawkers of a quantity like those who begin playing Christmas music in malls the week of Halloween so they can effectively compete with other shopping centers who are doing the same thing. Advent is not a chance for our church to get its slice of the season. It is a chance for us to affirm our partnership in the gospel.

For the next two weeks we will sing the carols of joy. We will light the candles on the Advent wreath. We will remember those who have labored with us on life's journey. All will not be perfect. The suffering and loneliness of this world will be very much with us. But, we hope, our partnership in that which began before our birth and continues beyond our death will remind us that Christmas is, indeed, a joy to be embraced instead of a problem to be solved. So be it.

---

1. F. W. Boreham, *The Blue Flame* (New York: Abingdon Press, 1930), pp. 27-31.

2. Raymond F. Collins, *Preaching the Epistles* (Mahwah, New Jersey: Paulist Press, 1996), pp. 9-11.

3. See the treatment by Fred Craddock, *Phillipians: Interpretation, A Bible Commentary for Teaching and Preaching* (Atlanta: John Knox Press, 1985), pp. 15-17.

4. Ben Witherington III, *Friendship and Finances in Philippi* (Valley Forge: Trinity Press International, 1994), p. 41.

Advent 3

Truce Or Peace?

Philippians 4:4-7

Now here's a Scripture with which we can all identify, especially during the holiday season. *Immediately* preceding the selected passage, two women are having a quarrel of some consequence in the Philippian church. The disputants are leaders in the church, which shows us that leaders are as capable of being petty as are non-leaders.

So, listen friends. Cast aside for a moment the beautiful gospel passage of sweet virgin Mary and her older cousin Elizabeth getting along fabulously together in their time of pregnancy. Put out of your mind the magi who travel like the three amigos, palatable comrades on a common quest. The lectionary lesson for today is as much a part of our season as any we have inherited. Paul is *pleading* with two individuals to agree with each other in the Lord. The early church, like our later church, is in as much danger of being victimized by its problems within as it is in danger from its problems with the outside world. Paul is pleading for peace!

Since it was customary for Paul's letters to be read aloud to the whole church in a worship service, the lesson apparently aims at much more than publicly embarrassing Euodia and Syntyche. Paul is speaking of rejoicing in the Lord and being guarded by a peace of God which transcends all understanding.

Perhaps many of us grew up in families where the best we could hope for during the Christmas season was an uneasy truce instead of a mysterious peace. In my family, Christmas meant a trip to Grandmother's house, three hours away. With the usual pettiness of children and the excitement over the season accompanying us, my sister and I presented quite a behavioral challenge to our parents. Usually a few stern rebukes and admonitions that we would receive no presents if we quarreled or "acted up" produced a *truce* among us until we returned home from Grandmother's.

In a strange way, warring cultures have historically observed uneasy truces during religious festivals. The fighting Greek city-states would hold a truce for the Olympic games held every four years in Olympia or Delphi. Preachers have for generations used to good effect in sermons historical illustrations of Confederate and Union soldiers good-naturedly tussling for a wild turkey during a Thanksgiving or Christmas truce. Even World Wars I and II held up their end of the bargain on occasions when Allied and German soldiers would sing "Silent Night" across the cold, quiet battlefronts of Europe. A truce is understandable. It is a lull between the fighting.

In our wealthy culture of diversions, would that we knew the things that make for peace. The text from Philippians was written to those who were religious. To them, preparing for the Lord's coming was a daunting task, a matter of dotting all the i's and crossing all the t's in life. Philippi was a wealthy city. In many ways it was Rome in microcosm. As part of a Roman province rebuilt by Augustus and populated with Roman soldiers, Philippi was given the legal character of a Roman territory in Italy, the very highest honor ever bestowed on a provincial city.[1] In many ways the Philippians were like us — they were too wealthy to have a deep faith! Unlike in the rest of the world, women in Philippi held high civic offices and served as priestesses in society at large. Money and social status enabled women to play prominent roles in early Christian congregations in Macedonian provinces. The Philippian church was, obviously, as socially diverse as any in early Christianity since in Greek and Roman oratory it was common not to mention women by name unless they were financially notable.[2] Like all good citizens then, as now, the Philippians understood truces, compromises, and appearances. But what about peace?

In our world many of us still do not understand peace as a mystery, a gift, that cannot be understood by the human mental capacity. To read Paul's letter one would think that Paul was in a happy place. Yet here was Paul chained like a criminal for his faith in Christ, waiting hour by hour for the door to open and for his persecutors to take him and execute him. How Paul could write, "Rejoice," is as much a mystery as the peace he so pointedly tried to articulate.

When I pastored a church in Texas, a man named Virgil Dunn was a member. Virgil was 93 years old when I knew him. He wore thick glasses and he spoke mainly in whispers. His body was thin and bent and his face was wrinkled. He and his wife lived in a small, white clapboard house. Virgil had been a member of that church all his life. He was kind, gentle, and radiant. He applied the love of Jesus to everyone he met.

Now, the church had a problem. Its former house of worship had not been used in over twenty years. It was falling down. The insurance companies had long since refused to insure it. Birds had built their nests in the pews and everyone was afraid to go in there. It just sat on a corner right in the middle of a major university, taking up space. It needed to be torn down. Several times people had almost come to blows in committee meetings over the issue.

One day a leader in the church came up to me. "Let's tear down the old church and make a park there in the middle of the campus," he suggested.

"Good Lord, we can't," I retorted. "Don't you know the history? One group of faculty and administrators will present a study claiming they know everything. Then another group will present a counter study showing *they* know everything."

"Well," he declared, "We've gone about it the wrong way. Don't claim to know *anything*. Just get Virgil Dunn to stand up there beside you and you report that we need to tear the church down. I'll make a motion. All Virgil has to do is nod. It'll pass if you have Virgil's presence."

A week later, we had the big vote. Virgil in his bottle thick glasses stood there beside me with a big smile on his face. When the motion was made, old Virgil nodded. It passed without a single negative vote. Not a negative word came back to us. We did not get a single ugly letter and the issue was never again discussed within the church.

It was the presence of a loving person that influenced the crowd. His presence helped effect a resolution that could not be planned for, could not be researched and anticipated, and could not be purchased. What's more, it could not even be rationally understood by anyone, including most of the faculty in the university's department of Religion and Philosophy, all Ph.D.'s, who were at the meeting.

As we look at our lives and our churches, what is it that gives us peace? If we take away the Scriptures, the logic, the talk, the manipulation, the budgets, the study groups, the music, and the sermons, all of which are great and good, is there a peaceful presence of Jesus Christ in *our* lives that guards our hearts and minds?

We live in a world of religious *shouters and arguers.* The airways are full of solitary individuals shouting "repent" to an indifferent world. The *shouters* are everywhere.

So are the *arguers* who want to evangelize by argument, smothering people with their logical scriptural traps, trying to win them over.

It seems amazing that Jesus lived on this earth for 33 years. Jesus and his disciples spent three years living together, traveling together, and working together. Yet if we were to take all the unduplicated words of Jesus in the Bible and record them, do you know how long the tape would play? Forty-two minutes! That's all. Forty-two minutes out of a three year ministry. Jesus left us 42 minutes of supposed direct quotes. He was the Son of God. Jesus influenced countless millions. But Jesus wasn't, apparently, much of a shouter and even less of an arguer. God's love is so wide, so growing, and so alive that it can't be limited or controlled by shouters and arguers. We don't have to pretend we know everything because God is always beckoning our hearts and minds to be controlled by a peace which transcends all understanding. This peace is much deeper than a truce between our arguments and shouts in God's behalf toward an indifferent world.

Sometimes we humans need to be confronted with the fact that the universals which unite the people on this planet are far greater than the particulars which we have allowed to divide us. Advent and Christmas are more than mere decoration and ornamentation on the backdrop of the ecclesiastical calendar. Advent and Christmas at their best take us into the hidden places of the human adventure where all languages and all symbols are transcended by a peace which cannot be fully understood. This peace, not a truce, makes no more human sense than did its first coming in the presence of the baby in a manger.

God certainly did not wait until the nations were at peace before sending the Christ to be born in Bethlehem's manger. God crashed the human experience when the prisoners were crying out for release and human need was great. Hearts were not pure and the world was tarnished with violence and doubt. Yet in joy, God came to live among us.

Neither can we humans wait until the world is in a human truce before we raise our songs of lasting joy.

The beauty and peace of Christmas are upon us in all their many expressions — music, paintings, symbols, stained glass, colors. The time is upon us, not for a truce amid the competing battles for our life's temporal allegiance, but a time for a peace that controls our hearts and minds. If Paul, writing from his jail cell to the Philippians is correct, then the peace of God which was in Christ Jesus is not a gift which a few people are given, but rather it is a gift which most people throw away.

What, then, begins for us this season — the world's way of truce or God's way of peace?

---

1. Ben Witherington III, *Friendship and Finances in Philippi* (Valley Forge: Trinity Press International, 1994), pp. 21-24.

2. A. J. Marshall, "Roman Women and the Provinces," *Ancient Society* 6 (1975), pp. 108-127.

Advent 4

Role Reversal: Baby And Priest

Hebrews 10:5-10

The university chaplain was late for a meeting. He roared down the interstate through a sparsely populated area of his state. He was traveling ten miles per hour over the speed limit. As the blue light from the highway patrol car flashed in his rearview mirror, the churning in his stomach was exceeded only by his anger at his foolishness. Putting on his best professional face and a humble demeanor, he gave the officer the requested information and jotted in his date book the time and location of his court appointment.

On the appointed day he journeyed to the rural, county seat town armed with a notebook full of excuses to try to impress the judge into letting this important man of the cloth out of his speeding ticket. His face turned an ashen gray as the proceedings began. The judge who walked into the courtroom and took his center stage seat was a former political science major at the university where the chaplain taught. Twenty years earlier the chaplain had given him a failing grade in a freshman religion course. With timidity the chaplain approached the bench. "I'm not going to get out of this, am I?" he meekly asked. "Not a chance!" came the reply. *Role reversal!*

Today's lesson is a necessary message for Advent. If understood, it means that we are not going to get out of this season merely focusing on the baby in the manger. Not a chance! Role reversal. Little Bethlehem has in its midst a small life, yet that body is being prepared for sacrifice as a great high priest.

The letter to the Hebrews suggests that the audience for this epistle were Jews. They would have been raised in the temple cult and attended that temple without fail on the Sabbath. They would have appreciated the role reversal in the letter. This Jesus, who attacked the temple and its priests, is pictured in the letter as the High Priest whose sacrifice (his bodily death) makes everyone holy.

Basic to an understanding of Hebrews is its view of salvation history. The old covenant with its law and cult is replaced by the new covenant which begins with the sending of the Son and his once-and-for-all-time sacrifice. The sacrificial cult is abolished by this new high priest who, by offering his life, completes the intention of the law. Role reversal! Good Friday becomes a nativity scene. There is no nativity scene without the shadow of the cross of Christ. The baby becomes the High Priest.

Advent is, indeed, a time of role reversal. During the rest of the year we preachers often attack the very commercialism we embrace during the advent season. The florist, who is the object of derision for society's penchant for spending lavish sums of money on cut flowers instead of memorials to the church, suddenly becomes our ever-present friend in a time of last-minute decorative need. The executive, whose income and life-style provide the meat for a few homilies on greed, becomes our number one hope for "making" the church budget. The cult of America's new religion, football, becomes the backdrop for our trips to college bowl games and ultimately climaxes down the road in our church super bowl parties or "souper" bowl emphases where we serve bowls of soup, for a hefty fee, to pump up the amount we give to benevolences. Our austere posture gives way to every special mission offering known to humankind. The sanctuary of the Christ, even in the most typically plain of churches becomes, for a time, the home to poinsettias, wreaths, colored candles, and Christmas trees. Role reversal! The baby has become the priest — if we can, to use Schweitzer's great image, see this Jesus as one who threw himself on the great wheel of history, determined to show humanity the kingdom of love and forgiveness lying crushed and lost within our social institutions.

Hebrews is a wonderful Scripture to move us beyond our infatuation with Jesus' stage of infancy and keep us from emphasizing the manger to the exclusion of the marketplace. It moves us from decorative concentration on the meekness of the baby into the marketplaces of life. It forces us away from buying gifts to celebrate a birthday and into a relationship with a priest who cannot be bought off with candy and flowers.

We can't get out of this easily, can we? Not a chance! The stockings hung by the chimney with care point to a body hung on a cross. The baby cannot eclipse the sacrifice of the man. Just as the Hebrews heard a Scripture which liberated them from their orientation to the old covenant with its law and cult, it might also give us a liberating thrust. Instead of a lowly baby meek and mild, we twenty-first century speeders through life stand before a High Priest who has already paid our ticket for us. This is, indeed, good news.

In his book *Dear Mr. Brown,* Harry Emerson Fosdick told of a father's desperate attempt to explain the nature of God to his young daughter, who was confused by the stories of war and destruction in the early part of the Old Testament. The father read from the later prophets: "What does the Lord require of you but to do justice, and to love kindness, and to walk humbly with your God?" Then he read from the New Testament: "Beloved, let us love one another, for love is of God, and he who loves is born of God and knows God." Presently the little girl responded thoughtfully: "Daddy, God grew better as he got older, didn't he?" That's one way of putting it. Another way is to say that God grows "better" as humans grow into a more mature knowledge of God's revelation. Indeed, God does grow in our minds. God is not an infant come to deliver a band of narcissists; God embraces the character of the man Jesus. God grows up and lives for those who grow up and live. Our defiled world reaches out for the spirit of the adult.

A marvelous image is thrust before our eyes. The corporate memory of those first Christian generations leaves us a vivid image of what it means to live as a Christian in any age. The corridors of time are crowded with men and women laboring under the weight of the laws of the world and their own experiences. Each awaits an appearance before the High Priest, the judge of their existence. Each in his or her own way has in hand the personal accumulations of a lifetime, hoping these little offerings of money, understanding, and trinkets will sustain them. Some are in agony, seeking to retain their faith and dignity in the face of crippling sorrow and a sense of loss. Some hope to survive the unbending rules of social structures which have disintegrated their courage. Some have been the butt of crude jokes.

Having been "flashed down" on the highway of life, yet trying to remain serene and controlled in the face of it all, we thumb through our briefcases full of excuses, offerings, cantatas, lists of good deeds and scraps of Scriptures, hoping our hearing will go well.

The great High Priest takes a seat as all rise. Papers in hand, we approach the bench in fear and trembling. The great High Priest glances down. "Don't need your offerings, though they helped your spirit," he calmly states. "Don't need your cantatas, though I enjoyed listening to them and they expanded your spirituality," he continues. "Don't need your scraps of Scriptures, though I am glad you memorized them," he adds. "Don't need your list of good deeds, though my beloved church and human need demanded them," he concludes.

The plaintive question shivers its way to the forefront: "I'm not going to get out of this, am I?"

Comes the response which reverberates its way across the corridors of time and the wreckage of human frailty: "Of course you are. I took all I had, even my life, and sacrificed it for you. You are holy and always will be."

Whew! Let Christmas come.

Christmas Eve/Day

Having To Stay When You Want Out

Titus 2:11-14

One of the difficult aspects for many people during the Christmas season is travel. Christmas is certainly no longer "over the river and through the woods, to Grandmother's house we go." Over fifty percent of all Americans now live over 500 miles from the place of their childhood roots. Going "home" for Christmas now means arriving at the airport an hour early, lugging presents to the UPS pick-up, renting a car, hoping you can get through the two-and-a-half hour layover in some big city airport, avoiding gridlock when passing near an urban metropolis, and wondering if you will have to spend the night in a train station as inclement weather backs up the schedule of an entire corridor of the country.

It's painful to have to stay in a strange place, far from home, when you really want to get out of there at all costs. Who hasn't waited in a tough place, trying to get home to celebrate Christmas?

Not all experiences with travel anxiety are physical. Every pastor knows what it's like to have to smile, put on a friendly face, and stay somewhere when you really want to leave. Can you imagine what it's like to attend a church reception being held in your honor to say, "Good-bye," to you when you are ready to leave for a new field of service? You don't want to go. Your spouse is feeling sad and you're often too dumb to realize all the sacrifices that you are laying upon your family. You pose for the pictures, pick up the "love offering" check, or hold the engraved silver tray, as you secretly wish you could be anywhere but there.

Can you imagine being the pastoral or liturgical head of a church, trying to go through the motions of the Christmas season with a congregation whose vision and needs are completely out of step with your own conception of ministry? You have managed to stay intact as a human being in spite of all the shaking of your spirit, but you know that inside the beautifully wrapped package you are a jumble of pieces of broken glass that resemble a hundred little pieces of confetti, held together by thin drops of ceremonial glue. You have to stay through it all when you really want out.

Sometimes the greatest messages about life are tucked away in rather obscure and unlikely places. Such is the case with the letter written to Titus. The letter was a response to some of Titus' complaints about Crete, the place Paul had assigned him. Titus hated Crete. He wanted to get out of there, and the sooner the better. Paul, or another author, responded with the pastoral epistle we now have. In essence, he told Titus that if Crete had not been a bad place there would have been no reason to send Titus there. "For this cause," said Paul, "I left you in Crete, that you should set in order the things that are wanting and search out good people in every city." That phrase, "For this cause I left you in Crete," is repeated several times in the introduction to this letter to Titus.

I can identify somewhat with Titus in that I have physically been to Crete. The trip there is a rough one. A depression in the sea produces high winds and lots of waves. One has to pass through the "graveyard of the Aegean" to get there. And the island peaked in 1100 B.C. A volcano blew up seventy miles north of Crete and literally leveled everything. Basically, the only real significance of Crete lies in the fact that the people there invented the safety pin and cremation. The weather there is brutally hot. I only spent the night there, and I wanted out of Crete.

The letter concentrated on the fact that happiness is not something you find but something you create. Titus had to discover his happiness in Crete. Titus had to turn difficulty into victory by following Christ.

If Titus was going to find happiness, he had to find it in Crete. He had to search out good people and cultivate their friendship. No one in Crete was going to knock on his door, barge in, and say, "Titus, let me make you happy."

Rabbi Beryl Cohon has been one of the most expressive thinkers in Judaism. Rabbi Cohon used to love to walk down the bank of the Charles River in the Cambridge-Boston area. One day he saw a number of boys sailing toy sailboats. They had seven little boats in the lagoon. Some were moving faster than others; one or two capsized and had to be pulled out and righted; one struck the embankment and had to be pushed off. Some barely had enough wind in their sails to drift along. A few were moving very fast. The same wind, blowing from the same direction, caused some to capsize, some to stall, some to move fast, and some to move in circles. They all were turning in different directions when the same force was playing upon all of them.[1]

The explanation, of course, lies in the set of the sail. As the sail is adjusted, so does the boat travel. If the wind is caught, the skillful sailor can even guide a vessel in the very teeth of the storm.

How do we draw from this Christmas season the strength to set our sail and remain upright in situations which threaten to capsize our spirits? It is precisely at this point that today's epistle proves instructive. The nativity of our Lord is forever linked to our baptism. Many interpreters view this lesson from Titus as reminiscent of ancient baptismal liturgies.[2] The author of the passage writes it in a single long sentence in Greek. Titus, in spite of his less than ideal situation, is being pointed to God's saving *grace* in Jesus Christ for all people. The emphasis is on how God's grace forms us. It is a saving grace because it teaches us to live as "self-controlled, upright and godly" people.

This ever-present grace, so available to Titus, is available to us all when we link our baptism to the nativity of our Lord. Our baptism, like our Lord's nativity, can withstand all the shakings of human history. It can, as it did for Titus, enable us to stay in situations from which there are no easy exits.

A young minister graphically described his involvement in an urban studies program which took him to the streets of San Francisco. One day he and several other ministers were instructed to put on worn-out shoes and old clothes and get into the line for free lunch at Saint Anthony's Dining Rooms.

The ministers moved along the line, exchanging nods with those who had to live for real the life the ministers were temporarily sharing. The ministers watched as the homeless people responded to each other, told stories, and scraped leftovers from others' plates into little plastic bags to have something to eat for supper.

Then, as the homeless people faded into the alleys and porticos of the city to return to their status as the lost and lonely, the ministers pulled off their dirty, ragged clothes and rejoined their instructors who had been involved in the same experience.

The meaning of the Christmas Event is most sharply defined at this point. We cannot discredit those who change from their identification with the poor and resume their middle-class life. Most of us wouldn't deign to dress down even one time.

L. D. Johnson posited that "the point of Christmas is that God came as Jesus Christ, 'born of flesh, born under the law,' as Paul put it, and *he stayed*."[3]

The epistle to Titus reminds him, and us, that the Christ has promised to stay always. The grace of God that first appeared in Bethlehem continues to "teach us" as we wait for the glorious appearance of our great God and Savior, Jesus Christ (vv. 12-13). The grace appears in the nativity of our Lord. It stays with us as a teacher. It will return to us in glory.

Titus rediscovered his Savior there in Crete. The *past* manifestation of God in Jesus of Nazareth and the *future* manifestation of God in hope and glory marked the boundaries of God's plan of salvation.

Today we celebrate the day of the birth of our Lord. The good news is the fact that our Lord *stayed* after the birth and will come to us again. So be it.

---

1. Beryl Cohon, *Out of the Heart* (New York: Vantage Press, 1957), p. 77.

2. E. Elizabeth Johnson, *Proclamation 6, Series C: Advent/Christmas* (Minneapolis: Augsburg Fortress, 1997), pp. 40-41.

3. I am the minister in the story and published it in Harold C. Warlick, Jr., *Conquering Loneliness* (Waco: World Publishing Company, 1979), pp. 11-12. L. D. Johnson responded to and used the story in L. D. Johnson (compiled by Marion Johnson) *Images of Eternity* (Nashville: Broadman Press, 1984), p. 54.

Christmas 1

The Next Step

Colossians 3:12-17

Paul's letter to the Colossians has a rhythm to it, "put out ... put on." It's a rhythm with which we contemporary Christians can resonate. There is a certain throwing away of past practices that eventuates in every productive life. One year I decided to use the time after Christmas to rid myself of my old clothes. With great zeal I threw the old, out-of-style ties, shirts, sweaters, and pants into the trash. Right there, amid the mangled and torn Christmas wrappings, the faded, dry greenery, and the cracked and broken decorations, sat my old clothes. They no longer served me. I no longer believed in them. They had failed to keep up with my needs and my desired personae. But, alas, my closet was then virtually empty. I had nothing to wear. Consequently I had to go shopping for an entirely new wardrobe. Trying to find something to "put on" was more expensive, tiring, and agonizing than tossing out the old attire.

To get rid of that which isn't wanted is fruitless if one does not take the next step and replace it with something that is much more effective.

To decide to stop paying rent is a momentous decision only if one is willing to take the next step and purchase a house. To remove a diseased limb is to leave one less than whole without a willingness to take the next step and undergo rehabilitation. To decide not to be single pales before the next step of committing oneself to being married.

It's always that next step that causes us to pause. We become like the crab that has moved out of its old shell, floating in a vulnerable, exposed state over the waters of existence, waiting on the next protective shell to cover our feebleness.

Life after Christmas is not all sweet. After our wonderful Christmas celebrations we are confronted with the fact that the Kingdom has not yet arrived. The week after Christmas is the anniversary of some less-than-angelic episodes in human history. The day after Christmas is when the church commemorates the death of Stephen, the first Christian martyr. Only two days after Christmas in 1941 the Japanese bombed Manila. On that same day in 1972 Soviet troops invaded Afghanistan. On December 28 back in 1890, the horrible battle of Wounded Knee took place on the American plains.

If we are going to put out the Christmas lights, we had better find some practical ways to turn on the lights of everyday kindness, for our world seems to need a witness in the days immediately following the putting away of the theoretical celebration of the nativity. Ringing out the old is but a prelude to a dangerous wrestling with the new.

Letting go of the old ways always creates the terror of embracing new ways. In Paul's wonderful letter to the Colossians he begins with a great house cleaning of old gods and old practices. "Let no one take you captive through hollow and deceptive philosophy"(2:8). "Do not ... do not ... put out ... put out." To a people obsessed with nature worship, astrological speculation, and wisdom teaching drawn from Hellenistic mystery cults, Paul was adamant: "Put out your old religious clothing. Get rid of the old. Don't live with excessive food, drink, sex, and mortification of the human body." The first half of the letter is a clear list of taboos. The old ways are dead. He talks constantly about the need for a "makeover." And if you are going to get a new image you've certainly got to strip away the old stuff you've gotten wrapped up in: "fornication, impurity, passion, evil, desire, greed, slander, anger, malice, and filthy language."

We can all understand that stripping away of our old ways. But what's the next step? What are the distinctive marks of the new face? Once before, in antiquity, the Jews had faced the issue of having to put out the old. Her promised land, her Davidic Covenant, her temple, and her old language of rewards and punishments had been rendered useless by the Babylonians. She had stripped away that old stuff as emblems of her faith. In her vulnerable and exposed state she had settled on two new badges of identification: circumcision and the Sabbath. And it had worked. Put out your old beliefs, put aside the Babylonian gods, and put on the new clothes of circumcision and observance of the Sabbath. It had worked and worked well.

Now, here are some new Christians in Colossae. Paul is not only telling them to "put out" their old gods and practices but to "put away," "put to death," "put off," even the old Jewish badges of separation, circumcision, and Sabbath. What, then, is the next step? What will be the new badge of identity? What shall we "put on"?

In a switch from his excessively negative language, Paul proceeds to talk about specific and down-to-earth ethical principles. Love is the Pauline badge of the new Christian profession. Everyday love is the next step.

It isn't enough to stop worshiping idols and refrain from evil. Throwing away an old and unclean garment is, indeed, necessary. The real kicker is putting on the virtue of love which Christ gave to us. And this love is something which must bind together every virtue, for it is not just in theory but in *deed*.

Some years ago a rather enterprising and effective public relations expert came up with the "What Would Jesus Do?" bracelet. Many Christians wore it as a trademark around their wrists. McDonald's had its "golden arches." Budweiser had its talking frogs. Christians had their "WWJD" bracelets.

Yet a trademark is but the first step. The next step is to improve the product. "What Would Jesus Do?" has to become "What Would Jesus Have *Me* Do?" Here is the genius of the great apostle. He writes the Colossians that they must let the "word of Christ dwell in you richly as you teach and admonish ..." (3:16).

Paul fully understands the transforming significance of the cross of Christ. It is not the "trademark" of a church that flies over the building or hangs from a golden chain around the neck of a believer. The love exhibited by God in Christ on the cross is a practical strategy for finding a new life.

The cross was used by the ancient Romans to put an end to political uprisings. They discovered that not only is a cross a slow and painful death, but it is also public. It would also serve as a deterrent to others. For the Jews the cross was an especially shameful thing. The Romans learned that in Jewish law a man being hanged from a tree was a curse by God. They seized on the perfect means to squelch trouble-makers in Israel. Hang them on a cross out there on the highway where everyone passing by would see them. If you had a problem with a group, the cross would make them scatter. Strike the shepherd and the sheep will run off. It would put an end to this Messiah business.

And it appeared to work. Jesus' disciples went into hiding. The empty tomb didn't make much difference to either the Romans or the disciples. Empty tombs were not that uncommon in those days. People were always stealing bodies. They said the same thing happened to Jesus' body. Somebody obviously stole it. An empty tomb was not impressive. It did not proclaim Jesus as resurrected. The cross did.

The cross came back, not as a curse but as a strategy for building a new world. Christians began to die the way Jesus did, loving those who were their enemies. Christians began to forgive people, in Jesus' loving words from the cross, for they did not know what they were doing.

The Romans made a big mistake. When everyone was scattered and wanted nothing to do with this Jesus, they let Mary Magdalene through the police line guarding the tomb. No one paid much attention to her. They just let her push up the yellow tape and head on. After all, she was a woman, which in those days and in that culture, meant that no one would take her seriously. She stayed there at the tomb and ran back to report what she saw.

It changed everything. The cross came back. Suddenly people were scratching it on coins over the face of the Roman emperor. People were painting crosses on the walls of their homes and in caves. People were using a cross as a strategy for building a better world. People were going to their deaths in the coliseum in Rome and making the sign of the cross and forgiving those who had done them harm. This was how the officials knew that Jesus was resurrected. They tried to get rid of Jesus with a cross. But they got both Jesus and the cross. They both came back

This was the message of Paul to Colossae: "Put out ... put on the cross of forgiveness in your everyday words and deeds." Take that next step beyond self-denial. Catch up the whole of life and place it under the aegis of the love of Christ.

Some years ago, the city of Atlanta went through the fight over whether or not to have a paid holiday for Martin Luther King, Jr. Atlanta settled for a supper of appreciation. Daddy King, Martin's 82-year-old father, had just gotten out of the hospital. He came to the supper from his home. He was weak, ate nothing, and scarcely talked during the meal. When most of the festivities were over, he was asked if he had anything to say. He shuffled to the microphone and this is what he said: "I'm old and I'm tired. And I'm sick. I've lost two sons and a dear wife — all too early. But I want you to know tonight that I hate no man. I hate no man!"[1]

If the forces of evil took away your children and your wife's bullet-ridden body were draped over your church's organ, could you get up and say, "I want you to know I hate no person"?

That's the next step: a higher motivation for life than self-denial and vengeance. Put out the harmful, the superstitious, and the false. They do not work. Take the next step. Put on the virtues of kindness, forgiveness, compassion, humility, gentleness, and patience. And over all these virtues put on love which binds them together.

---

1. As quoted by Thomas Conley, Northside Baptist Church, Atlanta, Georgia, September 21, 1986.

Christmas 2

A Secret Is Finally Revealed

Ephesians 1:3-14

Picture an attractive mother, a handsome husband, and three lucky children. The little children are fortunate because they have been adopted by the mother and father. The mother can not naturally bear children.

She had a bodily imperfection when she was born which resulted in her having had a colostomy, the process where you wear a bag with a tube to empty your wastes from your body. It was a most difficult and, obviously, painful condition with which to live. Consequently over the years the parents adopted two children. Then, last year, the mother had an ovarian tumor removed which was the size of a volleyball. That's when they adopted the third child.

In her college years the mother was the captain of the cheerleading squad at Duke University. The great Duke basketball team was charging its way toward a national championship under Coach K. when the Atlantic Coast Conference Championship rolled into the Greensboro Coliseum. Her minister was fortunate enough to secure a ticket to the Duke-Maryland game and took his seat in section 108. That section was full of University of Virginia fans. But Virginia did not play until the next game. The few hundred fans in that section were casually eating hot dogs, sipping overpriced soft drinks, and waiting through a game in which they had little interest.

The minister stepped into the aisle and looked down and got a big smile and wave from this Duke cheerleader. A nicely-dressed woman seated next to him noticed it and asked, "Is that girl a relative of yours?" He replied, "No, just a great friend and a great person."

Well, you know how the television camera person will pick out a pretty, athletic cheerleader to focus on during cut-aways throughout a game. The ESPN director chose her for obvious reasons. She was the prettiest. She was the most athletic. And her face radiated a sheer joy that just lit up the screen. As the game started and progressed, the cheerleader routines got more frenzied and complex. By the second time out the Duke pep band was playing faster and faster. The cheerleaders were into incredible dance steps, forward and backward flips, and body shakes and twists out at mid-court. The ESPN camera, with its long cable, was right out there at mid-court with the cameraman lying on the floor shooting the performance of this single girl.

The lady next to the minister leaned over and said, "Your friend is fabulous. She's amazing. I've never seen anybody dance like that. No wonder the national television crew is focusing on her. She's so radiant!"

"Yes," he exclaimed. "She's always been joyous. And it's amazing that she does all that despite having had a colostomy as a child. She will never be able to bear children."

It was like this lady had been hit between the eyes with a plank. Her face froze in total shock. "My God, you aren't serious," she declared.

"Yes," he stated.

A few seconds later the spectator whispered something to her husband and pointed down at the cheerleaders. He, in turn, tapped the man in front of him, whispered in his ear and pointed. The process went on until, after ten or fifteen minutes, everyone in section 108 knew the secret. By the start of the second half, section 108 was boisterously cheering for Duke. And every time the Duke cheerleaders ran onto the floor, section 108 stood, clapped and shouted.

These hundreds of strangers, whose names they will never know and whose faces they'll never see again, adopted other strangers for a brief period, as a family. They did this because of the joy and courage of one human being whose story they were able to share. They knew a secret others did not know.

Wouldn't life be wonderful and joyous if we could know a secret that would transform all the strangers around us into a family?

The writer of Ephesians made a powerful statement to the effect that none of us are natural-born children. We were all adopted. He stated that God, as an act of love, decided before time began to adopt everyone on earth through Jesus Christ and freely give us adopted children God's entire estate.

Most of us probably do not understand the seriousness of those adoption papers. We inherit everything God owns under God's last will and testament. We are the illegitimate children of the world who receive everything our creator leaves in the will.

The first Christians were acutely aware of the joy of being adopted. Under Roman law, adoption was a serious step. Copper money and scales were used. The biological father would put the child to be adopted on the scales and the adopting father would balance the scales with the child's weight in copper coins. That payment was the first step. Then the adopting father had to go to the magistrate and plead his case for adoption. When the adoption was completed, the adopted child had all the rights of inheritance in the new family. All the child's debts and obligations connected with the previous family were abolished, stricken from the records, as if they had never existed. You were, obviously, quite lucky if someone adopted you. You were doubly rich — your past was forgiven and your future held the promise of a powerful inheritance.

God, through Jesus, adopted us from a situation of loneliness, sin, and death, and gave us the potential to become a family again. Ezekiel, the great prophet, depicted Israel as an illegitimate child who, on the day of her birth, was cast into an open field and left to die of exposure. But God came by and adopted that foundling into God's family. That, said the writer of Ephesians, is what God did for the whole world, not just one nation, in Jesus. We were lying exposed in an open world, with all kinds of human obligations. Death was the lot to which we were born. We were not going to make it. But God adopted us, paid for us with God's only child, and gave us all there is to have.

Like the strangers to each other in section 108 in the Greensboro Coliseum years ago, we know a secret not everyone knows. Someone has tapped us on the shoulder and whispered, "God has adopted the world. We are God's children. Through the death and resurrection of Christ, we have been bought. Those strangers around us are our brothers and sisters." We participate equally in God's last will and testament.

Ephesians is one of the most positive books in the Bible. It is easily the most positive of the letters attributed to Paul. He is not on the defensive when he writes it. The letter is not even written to a particular church or to address a specific situation. It is an ecumenical letter intended for circulation among many churches in the area of Ephesus.

The letter is flooded with what Leonard Griffith calls "a deluge of affirmations."[1] Paul is telling these relatively new Gentile Christians that God has finally made known his hidden purpose, determined before creation, to adopt them through Christ.

This great affirmation was especially welcomed news to that entire group of churches. No group needed an everlasting identity more than did those new Asian Christians.

The first apostles tried to lend their names and their reputations to the churches in the Holy Land. They created apostolic churches. To be a bona fide apostle you had to have been with Jesus when he had lived on the earth. The Asians, on the other hand, possessed none of the big names and reputations. Jesus had not visited Asia Minor and Greece and places like Ephesus, Corinth, Sardis, Colossae, and Philippi. The Holy Land had the majority of the apostles, the majority of the places Jesus visited, and the majority of the money. Quite obviously, everyone focused on the New Jerusalem idea, the coming of the kingdom there. In fact, the apostles called the Greeks together and said, "We are the ones with the reputation and the history and the money. Majority and tradition rule. You fellows know it would not be right for us to wait on tables, take care of widows, and take precious time away from our valuable preaching, teaching, and praying. So you new fellows choose some people to do that and we'll lay our hands on them and set them apart for that. We will lend our reputations, *inheritance*, and names to the cause. You do the work and we'll stay here and lend our legacy to the churches of the Hebrews." It's all there in Acts 6:1-6.

To a divided and disordered world, including even these factions within early Christianity, Paul addressed his great affirmation.

God wanted to reverse the process and restore the original unity of creation. And this was no last-minute decision. God's invasion of the cosmos in Jesus Christ to unify the world was being worked out long before the laying of the foundation of the world. God had long ago determined that humans would need a savior. In short, you and I and these early Asian and Greek Christians were not last-minute additions to the plan. Our identity as adopted daughters and sons of God and our share in God's inheritance was not a codicil added to God's original "Jews only" testament. Jesus was a part of the plan since the beginning. And in Jesus, said Paul, we were "predestined" to be adopted as God's daughters and sons.

Now, we hope, this sermon has been progressing nicely to this point. But there is that confusing Presbyterian word "predestined" being used. Before the foundation of the world, God destined those first-century Asians and Greeks and you and me to belong to God as adopted children. Please don't confuse the concept with fatalism. Fred Anderson, pastor of Madison Avenue Presbyterian Church, New York, warns us that predestination does not mean that your life is pre-planned and there is nothing you can do about it. "Predestination is not about fatalism. It is about the love of God."[2] God, long before any human was born, destined us to be adopted because God is love and God has plans for us as God's children.

Paul's great affirmation provides what David Buttrick calls a "metanarrative,"[3] a universal concept that enables creation, fall, redemption, and glory to provide a meaning which sweeps across time. Without a sense of a meaningful future, a *telos*, those early Christians in the Ephesus region, not to mention you and I, would be given to short term goals. We would not appreciate the pervasiveness of the revealed secret.

We are all adopted children of God, paid for in the blood, tears, and sacrifice of a beloved son. It gives meaning to our future.

Dr. A. J. Cronin moved to this country and took up residence in Connecticut. He and his family had for their neighbors a family by the name of Adams. Henry Adams, the father, commuted to New York City every working day, where he was an accountant. He spent his weekends working in his little garden, accompanied by his only son, Sammy. When World War II began, Mrs. Adams suggested to Henry that they adopt a refugee. Henry was not enthusiastic about the idea but finally agreed to go along with his wife. Together they went to New York to pick up their refugee. He was a little boy from Central Europe, with the name of Paul Piotrastanalsis — an undernourished little fellow. They felt discouraged at first, but then when they began to feed little Paul a good diet, he became friendlier. The Adams family members became hopeful. But as the weeks passed, their hopes disappeared.[4]

As Paul learned the language, he began to lie incessantly. He began to steal. He displayed no affection toward either Mr. or Mrs. Adams. He was totally indifferent toward the mother and father. However, he did develop a deep friendship with little Sammy Adams.

One day, in direct violation of instruction, Paul Piotrastanalsis went swimming in a polluted stream. Paul came home with a raging fever. With the threat of contagion being so great, Paul was isolated in a well-equipped attic room. The parents feared his contacting Sammy. They warned him to stay there until the fever passed, and gave all the family members strict instructions not to visit Paul. They carried him through the crisis, but one morning Henry Adams went to call his son Sammy to breakfast. In complete horror, he found Paul asleep in bed with Sammy, breathing straight in Sammy's face. Four days later Sammy Adams was dead from the virulent infection.

With some indignation, Dr. A. J. Cronin wrote a letter to his neighbor Henry Adams urging him to get rid of Paul. Six months later Dr. Cronin returned from a stay in California and visited Henry Adams. As he approached the yard, he thought he was seeing ghosts. There in the garden was the familiar sight of a man and a boy working side by side. When he got closer he saw that the boy was Paul. "You still have him? You still have him?" Dr. Cronin asked in amazement.[5]

Henry replied, "Yes, and he is much better now. He is brighter and quieter." Henry Adams then stood up. "And, Dr. Cronin, you need not bother any longer trying to pronounce his name. He is now Paul Adams. You see, we have adopted him."

Cronin muttered, "All I can say to you, Paul, is that you are a mighty lucky fellow."

What a lucky person, indeed. And what a price the Adams family had to pay to rescue an individual from his own self-destructive tendencies.

Unbeknown to Dr. Cronin, it was destined to turn out that way for little Paul. The Adams family was a loving family. It had been that way from the beginning. The secret of their nature was finally revealed to their neighbor. They had *plans* for Paul Piotrastanalsis. So too, does God still have plans for you and for me.

---

1. Leonard Griffith, *Ephesians: A Positive Affirmation* (Waco, Texas: Word Books, 1975), p. 15.

2. Fred Anderson, "Discovering Your Destiny," *The Madison Avenue Pulpit*, 4 January, 1998.

3. David Buttrick, *Preaching the New and the Now* (Louisville: Westminster John Knox Press, 1998), p. 18.

4. As told by C. A. McClain in *Good News for Off Seasons* (Nashville: Abingdon Press, 1979), pp. 23-24, 31-32.

5. *Ibid.*

* If you are to this point in your quest for authenticity, you will note that in the first part of the sermon I refer to "the writer of Ephesians." In the middle of the sermon I purposely refer to "Paul's letter to the Ephesians." I am aware of debate as to whether Ephesians was written by Paul from a Roman prison or by a follower of Paul after Paul's death. When referring to the letter in general, I admit the difficulty. But the particular text used as the lesson for today certainly reflects Paul's theology, even if incorporated by a follower of his into a larger letter. Consequently I refer to it as "Paul's" affirmation.

Epiphany

From Crumbs To Half A Loaf

Ephesians 3:1-12

On a Boy Scout camping trip, the little group of scouts hiked up a mountainside and made camp for supper. They discovered that they were low on water. They had barely enough water to make a little stew. Two boys were sent to find water and fill the canteens while the others stayed and cooked supper. Unfortunately the two seekers were over three miles from camp when they finally located some water. The other boys gave up on them and ate all the stew. When the two returned to camp they were extremely hungry. So they went from boy to boy collecting the leftover pieces of bread they had on their plates. In essence, they found their nourishment in those collected bread crumbs. When you're in the wilderness and you're hungry enough, you'll eat anything. If your plan A (stew) has gone awry, you have no choice but to accept plan B, the leftovers.

A particular attitude is developed in the mind and soul of those who must accept second best. Their most acute problem is to deal with the estimate of their situation that the environment places on them. If they accept the judgment of the circumstances, they, like the two late-arriving Boy Scouts, are reduced to subservient bottom-feeders in order to survive. Yet mere survival is hardly the basis for developing an accurate and positive identity.

Some people tend to view the New Testament church as God's Plan B, the afterthought that had to be executed after Plan A (Israel) strayed off the mark. There is plenty of evidence from this perspective to make such a claim.

One of the most vivid images in the New Testament is that of the fascinating encounter Jesus had with the Greek woman who had a sick daughter. Jesus, to that point, had performed his miracles only with other Jews. He had fed 5,000 Jewish people on a hillside. Now he faced a crisis in his ministry. Here came a woman from a different race, a Gentile, a Greek. She was from a different religion. The woman asked nothing for herself. She was in a wilderness. Her daughter had a terrible debilitating illness and she sought only to help her daughter out of that wilderness of sickness and pain. Jesus at first rebuked her, saying, "Let the children first be fed (meaning the children of Israel) for it is not right to take the children's bread and throw it to the dogs (meaning the Gentiles)." But the lady would not be put off. She answered, "Yes, Lord; yet even the dogs under the table eat of the children's crumbs."

She begged Jesus for a few crumbs. In other words, her plea was this: "I don't want the whole loaf. You keep that for the main people. But please, please, dear God, if you are the bread of life, can't you at least throw some bread crumbs my way? Are there any bread crumbs for me?"

Jesus then healed the daughter and so began the ministry to the Gentiles, a ministry that changed the world. And it all started because a woman in the midst of her darkness, her wilderness, cried out for a little bread in the midst of her hunger. *Are there any bread crumbs for me?*

Today's lesson deals with this all-important issue: What is the relationship of the Gentile church to Israel? From crumbs to half the loaf is a leap, especially in a writing in the name of one historically known as an arch-persecutor of the church. When today's lesson is juxtaposed with the story of the Syro-Phoenician woman (Mark 7), an epiphany takes place. "A dramatic shift has occurred in the history of salvation."[1] Like all true epiphanies, darkness gives way to light, mystery to revelation, and ignorance to knowledge. The Gentile believers in the Messiah, Jesus, are co-heirs of the messianic promise that reaches back to Abraham.[2]

Good news is apparent in the text which clearly states that Gentiles have become fellow heirs, members of the same body, and sharers in the promises of God. Those who once begged for crumbs now are revealed to own an equal share of the whole loaf. The new has not replaced the old; the fruit has simply ripened on the tree. The mystery has been revealed. The roots silently at work in the depths of Jewish tradition are now above ground and growing. That the Gentiles are now part of the same body with Jewish Christians makes Christ the hinge on which a new world is being created. A new world is being born.

The revelation of the "mystery" starts with a request to Jesus for "crumbs" of bread. It continues in the autobiographical portions of today's lesson. Paul's life is depicted as being a prisoner of Christ, not of empire. The text goes on to direct us to think of the manifestation of Christ to the nations through the mission of the church. It concludes with a depiction of a cosmic epiphany.

The mystery is not only revealed to humans. It is also revealed to rulers and authorities in heavenly places. There is no longer any reason to fear the forces of hate and determinism which shackle modern Americans as much as Hellenistic believers in heavenly powers. Even the demonic and heavenly realms are made aware that things have changed.

From crumbs to half a loaf — co-inheritors; the news reached cosmic proportions. The writer of Ephesians makes it clear that this is not just a message of good news to one people in one earthly time span. It is an assault on the heavens as well.

A little five-year-old boy once sat in despair in his hospital room. He was dying of cancer. Within a matter of hours he would be gone from this earth. The theology students were there, observing and taking notes on what children do when they die of cancer. The doctors and psychiatrists were there. His parents were there. All were analyzing, researching, comforting, and seeking to be profound. They were not experiencing much success. The little boy had not smiled much, his life a fairly constant barrage of needle pricks, medicine, and tubes. But sometimes the meaning of life and death is best uttered in the clear, succinct words of a child.

The medical history contained a report that the little boy had had a special friend, an older relative named Julie, who had died a few years before. After all the "comforters" had wound down their conversations and note-taking, someone finally asked him, *"What can we do that you would like, after you die?*" With a radiance befitting a rising sun, his face lit up and a broad smile took possession of his face. He very clearly said, "Put me in an ambulance, cut on all the lights and blow the siren as loud as you can — so Julie will know I am coming." And that's exactly what they did.

The letter to the Ephesians contains some magnificent words. It says that God was revealing a mystery that had been hidden for ages. "Through the church, the manifold wisdom of God would be made known to the principalities and powers in the heavenly places" (Ephesians 3:10). Not just on the earth, but in the heavenly places as well.

Those who started with the crumbs of Christ now own half the loaf. Such is the claim an amazing apostle stakes against both the world and the heavens. It is the water mark above which no tide of despair, suffering, and evil can rise.

Shouldn't that epiphany make us want to get on with our mission to the world?

---

1. See Fred B. Craddock, John H. Hayes, Carl R. Holladay, and Gene M. Tucker, *Preaching Through the Christian Year* (Valley Forge: Trinity Press International, 1994), p. 71.

2. Ralph P. Martin, *Ephesians, Colossians and Philemon: Interpretation* (Louisville: John Knox Press, 1991), p. 41.

Epiphany 1
(Baptism Of Our Lord)

The Scattering Of Lesser Figures

Acts 8:14-17

A certain physician started to practice medicine in a large city. His ambitions were strong and opportunities seemed plentiful there. Success was his right from the start. His practice became almost too large for him to handle. Fame and praise were heaped on him to overflowing. But he forgot that a doctor should do more than heal sick bodies. For this physician, a patient was only interesting if the sickness was interesting and then only as a stimulus to further his fame.

One day the prominent doctor got a letter from his best friend. The friend knew the doctor's reputation and begged him to come to the small town where he lived and try to save his sick little boy. When the letter arrived the doctor was engaged in some research work that could make him famous. He delayed his departure for a few days to complete his valuable research. When he finally arrived in the little town, he was too late. His friend's little boy was dead.

The doctor struggled long and hard with his emotions. His pride had made him a traitor to friendship and service. Gradually he began to develop a new mental attitude of love and service. He resigned his city practice and moved to the small town, becoming a lesser figure in his profession.

On a visit back to the city one day he encountered a puzzled colleague. The colleague could not understand how he could be satisfied with burying himself in a small town, denying himself a place in the sun. The good doctor confessed that his fame had eroded. Certainly there would be no great monuments erected in his honor and no big speeches by important people at his funeral.[1]

He was, indeed, a lesser figure on the world's stage of medicine. But his life, he believed, had been a success because he had felt a need to live for others and because love had entered into his life.

A unique aspect of Holy Scripture is the way it weaves together life narratives to convey to its readers essential truths about themselves and their world. As we look at today's text, its unspoken objective is to provide us with an appropriate interpretation of our own lives. The story of Philip among the Samaritans possesses all the ingredients necessary to bring truth to lesser figures like you and me. The text is not an abstract about inclusivity. It is a story which addresses our sins and fears and our hopes and experiences. You and I are lesser figures. We will not be the world's shakers and movers. We will not write the best-sellers, preach before the throngs in leading pulpits, discover the great cures, and become parents of the Academy Award winning actress. Most of us, wildly chasing our dream of bigger places and larger arenas, will, perhaps, wrestle most with the twin sins of our existence: wanting what we do not have and fearing that we will lose what we do have.

Here, then, is the appropriate Scripture for us lesser figures. It speaks of the preaching of Philip which contained a huge deficiency. His preaching was not accompanied by the gift of the Holy Spirit. Elsewhere in Acts all the other preachers seemed to have given the Holy Spirit to their converts as soon as they baptized them. What's more, Philip, who carried the gospel beyond the big city of Jerusalem, is a lesser figure who received the apostolic imprint. Along the way he encounters a magician named Simon who is so powerful all the people flock to him for his fame. And this same Simon wants to know how much it costs to buy the Holy Spirit, only to be shown that it is a free gift. The story in a very real way points out what usually happens when the gospel is scattered among lesser figures far away from its home base, in this case, Jerusalem.

Perhaps you and I cannot identify with Moses among the Egyptians, Jesus before the Sanhedrin, or Paul before the Athenians. But we scattered, lesser figures have all the elements of our lives there in Chapter 8 of Acts as we encounter Philip among the Samaritans.

That the gospel ever got out of self-centered Jerusalem was itself something of a major miracle. Pascal was fond of saying that it is the pathetic fate of God to be everlastingly misunderstood. Heavenly oracles and prophetic words, such as Jesus' great commission to go into all the world, are usually misconstrued by humans.

"Scatter!" said God to the first family. And Cain built a city! To a later generation God said, "Scatter!" and they built a city with a tower that tried to reach into the heavens! "Scatter!" said God to Abraham, "and in you all the nations of the earth will be blessed." And Abraham and his sons equated the message with their own little nation. "Scatter!" said God to the descendants of Moses. "And occupy the promised land I have given you," and they ransacked the mines and quarries of the whole earth to build a Temple of the Lord and royal palaces in one central spot! "Scatter!" screamed God through the prophets. And the priests dug up (or created) a long-lost(?) book called Deuteronomy during a Temple renovation project which enabled them to go out in the countryside and slaughter 300 rural priests and destroy their shrines in the name of "morality" and "progress!"

Then came God to earth. "Scatter!" he urged. "Go into all the world and preach the gospel to every creature." But all the world to them meant the little territory lying around the Mediterranean.

"Scatter!" urged the Christ. The gospel was meant to be preached to Gentiles (and Samaritans) as well as Jews. And his followers created the Apostolic Church through which every Scripture had to pass for approval or editing!

In the words of F. W. Boreham, "The Catholicity of a magnificent purpose was strangled by the parochialism of a conservative race."[2]

Today's text is a text laced with extremism. It probably shook its first century hearers more than it shakes us for we are quite comfortable with our parochial spirituality and see the Holy Spirit as something that can be purchased, if not with money, then with prayer and meditation. We tend to focus on the instruments of the Holy Spirit, holding up our favorite passages of Scripture to justify our liberality or our fundamentalism. We use our gothic facades, stained glass, and booming choirs to create an ambiance that arrests the spirit on one hand, while also acquiescing to the contemporary, hand-clapping shouts and rhythms of Generation X in our early-morning services. We are the magicians of our day. Like Simon, the magician, we want to know, "What's the cost so I can have this power, too?"

A great violinist was scheduled to play a concert in Houston, Texas. The Houston newspaper, however, didn't focus on the artist. It used most of its space to describe his original Stradivarius violin. In fact, the morning of the concert, the front page carried a picture of the great instrument he would play. That night, the hall was filled with people. The musician played extremely well. As he finished, the crowd thundered its applause. When the clapping subsided, the musician carefully laid his bow down. He carried a chair to center stage. Raising his violin over his head with both hands, he slammed it across the back of the chair. The violin smashed into dozens of pieces. The audience gasped. Walking back to the microphone, the artist said, "I read in this morning's paper about how great my violin was. So I walked down the street to a pawn shop. For thirty dollars I purchased a cheap violin. I put some new strings on it. That's the violin I played this evening, then smashed. I wanted to demonstrate that it isn't the violin that counts most. It's the hands that hold the violin."[3]

In this image-conscious world you and I need to pause every now and then and reflect on the God who inspires our faith and is the reason for the existence of our churches, our Bibles, and our hope for eternal life.

The Holy Spirit moves through people at God's discretion. There is no formula that can be evoked to get it. It is a divine gift. Some commentators[4] focus on today's text and maintain that it means the church should rebuke and exclude "those like Simon who did not change their heathenish lifestyle and attitudes."

Actually, it seems the Holy Spirit held back from offering itself because Peter and John (read the Church) had not obeyed Jesus' command to serve as his witnesses to Samaria. Part of Jesus' great commission was that they were to testify in Samaria. Yet it was not the church that took the message of Jesus to Samaria, it was the Hellenist Philip. The Samaritans believed him and were baptized.

But the Holy Spirit held back and *forced* the apostles to come and bless the Samaritans.[5]

The Holy Spirit seems to have rebuked the church for its parochialism. Since Peter and John preached the gospel in "many Samaritan villages" on their return to Jerusalem, one might say Peter and John appeared to have taken their own advice to Simon and repented of their own bitterness! Crazy things happen to God's word when "lesser figures" like Philip and you and I try to carry it beyond the boundaries of our own search for comfort and ease.

Thank God for the scattering of lesser figures.

---

1. This story was compiled by William Vickland, lay minister of the Little Brown Church of the Air, WLS, Chicago. It was printed in *The Little Brown Church of the Air, Sermon Stories*. The Reilly and Lee Company, Chicago, pp. 154-157. I have transposed the story into my own words and summarized its narrative.

2. F. W. Boreham, *The Blue Flame* (New York: Abingdon Press, 1930), pp. 220-223. His chapter, "The Instinct of the Circumference," was most useful.

3. As told in Herb Miller, *Fishing on the Asphalt* (St. Louis: CBP Press, 1987), pp. 32.

4. My colleague Will Willimon is the author of this quote as he calls attention to "the church demanded reprentance" in 8:22, in *Acts: Interpretation — A Bible Commentary for Teaching and Preaching* (Atlanta: John Knox Press, 1988), p. 70.

5. Marion Soards, Thomas Pozeman, and Kendall McCabe make this observation in *Preaching the Revised Common Lectionary* (New York: Abingdon Press, 1994), p. 102.

Epiphany 2

What Are Spiritual Gifts For?

1 Corinthians 12:1-11

A most important discovery has been made about trees. Derl Keefer[1] states that scientists have found that when the roots of two trees touch, there is a substance present that reduces competition. An unknown fungus helps link roots of various trees, including dissimilar species. In this way a whole forest can be incorporated together. With certain trees having access to nutrients, other trees access to water, and still other trees access to sunlight, possessing the means to cooperate with one another is essential. The purpose, of course, is not cooperation but to survive and grow!

Today's text is one that is familiar to many. Often there is a great desire to speak on the types of spiritual gifts and answer questions about their authenticity. Paul gave us a priority ranking of the list of spiritual gifts. Certainly Paul's reminder to the Corinthians about their earlier pagan days and the emotional practices of the mystery cults interests preachers. The placement of the gift of tongues in the last position also commands a lot of "air time" in pulpits. We all want to make certain we are dealing with people who are in contact with God and not their latent childhood fears, infantile needs for parental authority, or sweaty, adolescent emotionalism. Fine. Authentic spirituality is a real concern in contemporary American culture. Books about angels and Armageddon sell quickly and often. Most people who don't belong to a church still consider themselves to be "very spiritual." Consequently it is most tempting to view Paul's words as an appeal for cooperation and leave the message there. Actually, the divisions in Corinth are probably centered around competing house churches instead of individuals within a single church.² Corinth was a large city and easily could have had anywhere from six to twenty private homes among Christians that were sufficiently large enough for casual assembly and meal preparations (kitchen and dining room).

Has Paul required cooperation? Most assuredly. Yet cooperation alone is not his total focus. Unlike trees in a forest, churches are supposed to do more than link together and live. This passage is about more than keeping discord at bay or warning household units about trying to invalidate the spiritual perspectives of their neighboring unit a few blocks down the street.

Mark Twain told of being disturbed at all the discord he saw among God's creatures. He decided to experiment with the problem. He put a cat and a dog in a cage. He wrote that within an hour he had taught the cat and the dog to be friends. In another hour he added a rabbit and taught all three to be friends. Within several days he was able to add a fox, a goose, a squirrel, and some doves. Finally, he added a monkey to the mix. They all lived together affectionately.

Next he decided to experiment with religion. In another cage he confined an Irish Catholic, a Scotch Presbyterian, a Muslim, a Methodist, a Buddhist, and a Salvation Army Colonel. He stayed away for two days and came home to record the results. Not a single specimen was left alive.³ This tongue-in-cheek story resonates well with conditions in our world.

Certainly the creation of a church that loves and cares about others, regardless of who they are and what spiritual gifts they bring to the fellowship, is an important part of Paul's concern. Corinth, for all its secular and religious problems, was a place that was blessed. Its people brought to any endeavor a fine array of spiritual blessings, from knowledge to preaching to ecstatic tongues. Yet Paul is addressing a weightier issue: how will your gift build up the body of Christ? These things can be a blessing or a curse. Do they build up, edify, and serve the body of Christ? Paul begins his message by acknowledging that people can actually curse Jesus through spiritual speaking. How can one be "speaking by the Spirit of God" and say, "Jesus be cursed"?

Here Paul is setting up the next portion of his argument, one that will lead to his great metaphor of the one body and its many parts. Paul is concerned that the new Christians not return to their pagan ways, when they were led astray to "mute idols." These new Christians knew how to cooperate and have fellowship from having belonged to the various voluntary associations, philosophical schools, and households which were part of the Corinthian world. Paul is not as concerned with the *means* by which the Christian community is founded as he is with its purposes. This concern parallels, interestingly enough, our contemporary concern with so-called New Age spirituality.

Charles Allen, the great Houston, Texas, pastor, used a technique many ministers have alluded to in their efforts to travel. Sometimes on an airplane you just want to be left alone. Allen, when he didn't want to be pestered by fellow travelers seated next to him, employed a simple procedure. He would take out a Bible, open it, and place it in his lap. Everyone would leave him alone. The travelers didn't want to get in a religious discussion. But that was in the 1970s and 1980s.

Try that ploy today and things would probably transpire in a different manner. Most probably the person next to you would lean over and say, "I am very spiritual myself." Were you to ask that person, "Well, what church do you belong to?" you might be surprised. "Oh, I don't belong to a church. I'm just very spiritual."

Mute idols? Mute idols are idols which have no purpose other than being privately adored by their worshipers. Transcendental meditation is a wonderful exercise. But it makes a mute idol when trying to serve as an individual's deity. Celtic harp music is relaxing. But it is a mute idol against injustice.

The pagan Corinthians had had much experience belonging to households, mystery cults, philosophical schools, and voluntary associations where they ate meals, discussed their trades, and were made to feel good. Paul needed both to bring together a people with many valuable gifts and get them to begin reflecting on their larger purpose, doing something as a Body of Christ.

Bob Ferguson, a South Carolina pastor, has called attention to one of the most interesting developments of our time — Velcro. In the early 1940s, Swiss inventor George de Mestral went on a walk with his dog. Upon his return home, he noticed that his dog's coat and his pants were covered with cockleburs. His inventor's curiosity led him to study the burrs under a microscope, where he discovered its natural hook-like shape. This was to become the basis for a unique, two-sided fastener — one side with stiff "hooks" like the burrs and the other side with the soft "loops" like the fabric of his pants. The result was VELCRO® brand hook and loop fasteners, named for the French words "velour" and "crochet."

Most of us are grateful for Velcro. It easily brings things together and keeps them secure. Yet it is not the bringing together of disparate parts that is the wonder of Velcro. One might say that since it was invented nearly sixty years ago it was a "mute idol" for much of its life. Its invention certainly solved a problem and gave its inventor great satisfaction. But it was only when it was put to its purpose, hooking together shoes, holding computers, fastening together hospital implements, and you name it, that it made a difference in our world. How wonderful that one side of the gift with its stiff "hooks" could come together with the other side of the gift, its soft "loops." That mutual joining together was an essential first step. But we are grateful for Velcro due to the many ways its fastening capability has been put to use.

Many of you have been blessed with spiritual gifts. Cooperate with other Christians and other churches which have been blessed with spiritual gifts different from your own. But after the cooperation, go another step. Live out the kingdom model of unity and also live out the kingdom model of mission and service to a world that needs it so desperately. We are to use the Holy Spirit's gifts to us not only to build up the church, but to make this world a better place for the people for whom Christ died.

We sometimes forget just how primitive was the organizational structure of the early church. They had no statements of faith.

Paul is writing to a people who have nothing but a story that was transmitted orally and evidence of how his life was changed by God through belief in that story. All the sacred Christian traditions and places are way over in Palestine. Consequently his writings are a theology in process.

We have something in common with the early Corinthians. We have never seen Jesus and have never known anyone who has. But we have seen Jesus in the lives of people.

We cooperate too little over our boundaries and "isms." Getting together people who possess different spiritual gifts is still not easy. The next step, once that is done, is to behave and act in such a way that there is no other explanation for our attitudes and behavior except the Christ.

---

1. Derl Keefer *The Abingdon Preaching Annual 1998* (Nashville: Abingdon Press, 1997), p. 56. Thanks to Gary Carver of Chattanooga, Tennessee, for pointing me to this source.

2. Richard S. Ascough, *The Formation of Pauline Churches* (Mahwah, New Jersey: Paulist Press, 1998), p. 6.

3. This story from Mark Twain is printed in Jana L. Childers and Lucy A. Rose, eds., *The Abingdon Women's Preaching Annual* (New York: Abingdon Press, 1996), p. 128.

Epiphany 3

Respect

1 Corinthians 12:12-31a

Roland and Elizabeth were unusual guests at the complimentary "high tea" being held late in the afternoon in the four-star, luxury inn on Hilton Head Island. For one thing, Roland and Elizabeth were not guests of the hotel. They lived about twenty minutes away from the inn. Their home was in the wealthiest neighborhood on that island of very wealthy residents. In fact, Michael Jordan, the basketball legend, had lived next door to them. But Michael had stopped visiting the home after his father died.

Roland and Elizabeth had moved south a few years earlier to escape the harsh climate of western New York, near Buffalo. When they finally moved into their posh dream house, they noticed something unusual. They missed one of the very things they had taken for granted: neighbors. Virtually all the homes around them were expensive second homes for millionaires in Atlanta and Washington. No one was ever in their neighborhood longer than it took to spend a few nights and play golf and tennis.

So it was that Roland and Elizabeth came to pay a fee to the inn to allow them to come over once or twice a week and have tea with the guests. Roland and Elizabeth, out of their desperation, cared little where the strangers were from, what religious or political views animated from their one-day-stand comrades, or what personal or spiritual gifts were in the possession of their table guests. Roland and Elizabeth just wanted a little community, for however fleeting a moment it could be theirs.

How those things we take for granted can flare up and rob us of the essence of life. Most of us do not think of our body parts until they are sick or missing. Who focuses on his or her inner ear until it gets messed up and causes dizziness? No one thanks God for a healthy gall bladder until it gets diseased. In our ignorance about our body, we are perfectly happy until one of its parts begins to hurt. Then it dawns on us how important that part is, both physically and psychologically, to our well-being. Regardless of the infinite variety of parts that compose our bodies, whatever is hurting at the moment becomes the indispensable center of attention. We will pay any price to strangers who can offer us relief.

Paul immediately got the attention of the diverse Corinthians by talking about their bodies in relationship to forming a community. Roman and Greek orators had used the same image to speak about the State so the Corinthians were comfortable thinking metaphorically about the human body. The body and its limbs had been used by Roman senators with the Plebeians, and the Stoics had put the metaphor to good use in their political arena. This image was always a good one to drag out when trying to express unity and tolerance.

Christianity was not unique among religions in appropriating the image of the body and its limbs to express the work of the Holy Spirit in creating unity, a sense of togetherness, amid diverse members of a group. In the Mahayana Buddhist tradition each member was said to be like a hand or a leg of the Buddha: "The right hand never says to the left hand, 'I am doing charitable work for you.'"[1]

Certainly in the church every member is a part of the body of Christ. What is Paul really after? At first glance one might be tempted to say, "Tolerance," and let it go at that. Tolerance, unity amid diversity — certainly a worthy goal. And the crazy Corinthians could use all the tolerance for other people's religious gifts they could muster.

Paul is after more than tolerance. Way deep down, behind the flowing pen of his composition, is a clarion call for respect. Respect is quite different from tolerance. Stephen Carter in his work, *The Culture of Disbelief*, has noted, "Tolerance without respect means little."[2] If we tolerate someone's spiritual gift then it is our forbearance, not our recognition of the equality of that other gift, that allows the person possessing it to be a part of the church.

Toleration means only allowing something to exist. For many people the idea of toleration is bound up with the notion that those with different spiritual gifts will, in time, come to confess the error of their ways.

Paul's great description hammers home through the simile of the human body that each of us is *necessary* for the good of the Body of Christ. None of us has all the truth. We are a mixed bag of the necessary. When each part has equal concern for each other so that all suffer if one suffers and all rejoice when one is honored, that is respect.

Respect for that which is different seems to be the defining mark of Paul's entire ministry. The gifts he identifies among the Corinthians seem almost to be in conflict with each other, but we need to respect them all for we need them all in order to be the Body of Christ. When Jesus thought of community, he did not conceive of it as having "high tea" with strangers. His members were not to be desperate seekers after one-day (albeit a sacred day) stands with table guests. Nor were these Christians to be dues-paying members of a comfortable and secure group who had retired from the inclement weather and nasty pace of a secular world to gather with like-minded people for pleasant conversation.

In the first struggles of the infant Christian Church to embody the life of Christ, Paul takes it upon himself to articulate Christ's *respect*, not tolerance, for those who are different. The text challenges us to respect one another in our different places with our different gifts. And with respect comes the willingness to support and undergird one another. The world has seen tolerant religious groups before. But true examples of fellowship and love are rare, even in religious circles. They produce a body of mutual respect quite unlike that which is normally seen, even in a democracy such as ours.

Paul appeals to more than a worldly model of unity. This is no warmed-over Roman or Stoic appeal to tolerance. The whole body has to be well in order to function or that body will die.

The inventory of gifts is not important. What is important is that the old way of tolerance is past. The new way of respect for those who are different has broken upon the world through the

Holy Spirit. Respect for one another within the church becomes the catalyst for the way the Holy Spirit operates beyond the walls of the church.

Paul's statement about the different spiritual gifts had as its ultimate dream a day when it would not be necessary to speak of spiritual gifts at all.

Paul possessed a throbbing concern. He enabled the church to draw upon the Hellenistic notion of *paideia*[3] as a model for its life. Paul's letters were "teaching sermons." They were poised to form the character of their hearers and not just transfer information. The great apostle strove to enculturate a habit of thinking about the world in light of the community's deepest values which would allow the Christian to perceive and act for the good of all in any situation.

If respect for those inside the diverse church at Corinth could become the deepest value, then Christians could experience a profound conversion that would enable them to hasten the day when the whole of humanity would respect and love one another instead of compete in the market place.

What about our church? We are tolerant. But do we have respect?

People who have no sense of being an object of respect are seriously handicapped in making someone else an object of their respect. The person who has grown up feeling outside the reach of other people's respect has a dual handicap. On the one hand, he or she is quick to pass a judgment on himself which insists on his own unworthiness. At long last he feels rejected. On the other hand, the person may make an inner compensation for the lack of respect others show him. He or she becomes preoccupied with his own needs and interests. It can make such a person thoroughly self-centered and arrogant.

When a climate of acceptance is transformed into a climate of respect, we call that the work of the Holy Spirit. When that transformed climate becomes the dominant value of a group, we call that group the Body of Christ. When that body exists together through time, we call that body the Church!

So be it.

1. Thich Nhat Hanh, *Living Buddha, Living Christ* (New York: Riverhead Books, 1995), p. 67.

2. Stephen L. Carter, *The Culture of Disbelief* (New York: Basic Books, 1993), p. 3.

3. See Ronald J. Allen, *The Teaching Sermon* (Nashville: Abingdon Press, 1995), pp. 14-15, for an excellent analysis of the Hellenistic notion of *paideia*.

Epiphany 4

Old Favorite

1 Corinthians 13:1-13

Most of us play favorites, whether we admit it or not. All parents try to love their children with equal devotion. That's hard to do. My own parents had a favorite: it was my sister, I'm convinced. Yet from her incorrect perspective, I was the favorite. Favoritism seems to be a part of our biblical perspective. Abraham and Sarah favored Isaac over Ishmael. Then old Isaac favored Esau the country boy, but his wife Rebekah favored pompous little Jacob. There's no doubt old Jacob himself later favored and spoiled little Joseph. Most of us would say that the true course of action for a parent would be to love and favor the child that needs it most at the time.

Even preachers play favorites when it comes to certain Scriptures for sermons. Fortunately, some preachers use a lectionary and move through the whole Bible, but it's still hard to generate enthusiasm for an obscure sermon on the Rechabites, whoever they were. One preacher always listed a different sermon topic, but every Sunday you knew he was going to preach on John 3:16 and money, and use the feeding of the 5,000 by Jesus with a few loaves of bread and some fish as a climactic illustration. The congregation contended that he had but one sermon, on tithing, which he could preach in 52 different ways in a year's time.

Sometimes we hear messages that are so familiar they cease to have an impact on us. Just as a child gets spoiled from too much attention, too much favoritism, so do some of our Scriptures get spoiled. They are so familiar they get taken for granted and rush past us. We repeat the Lord's Prayer or the Ten Commandments with hardly a second thought. At funerals the preacher reads the twenty-third Psalm, and the mind seems to click to automatic pilot well before the preacher gets to the part about "walking through the valley of the shadow of death."

Today's Scripture *is* an old favorite. It's an old favorite that for many of us has become spoiled. Since childhood, most of us have heard the words of Paul's treatise to the Corinthians on "love." When a man went to talk to his future father-in-law about marrying his oldest daughter, he was a little nervous, to say the least. He just wanted to get his quick permission and get out of the den as quickly as possible. After all, no father thinks any boy is good enough to marry his daughter. And nothing is ever as simple as it first seems. So the young man had to sit there and listen to the venerable old lawyer's philosophy of life. The old clichés whizzed past his head like a rocket in flight. Finally, the elder gentleman concluded, "And be sure to read together 1 Corinthians 13 at least once a week."

1 Corinthians 13. That's like reading yesterday's newspaper for most of us. Old news. A sugar stick from a previous era.

But it's a genuine mistake not to re-examine, occasionally, the abiding significance of this old favorite. Most of us are familiar with the tragedy that grows and festers from lack of love. The examples are everywhere. So many people could have been different if they had but known love. The scenarios saturate even our American history. He began his life without love. His mother was a powerfully-built, dominating woman who found it difficult to love anyone. The mother gave her child no affection, no love, and no training during those early years. He was absolutely rejected from earliest childhood. Despite a high IQ, he was ugly and poor and unlovable. When he was thirteen years old, the school psychologist commented that he probably didn't even know the meaning of the word "love." His mother even forbade him to call her at work.

He finally dropped out of high school in his third year. He thought he might find acceptance in the Marine Corps. But his lack of love went with him. He was thrown out and laughed at, with an undesirable discharge. A young, scrawny man in his twenties with no sense of worthiness, he went to live in a foreign country. But he found no love there, either. He married a girl, who had herself been an illegitimate child, and brought her back to America. She developed the same contempt for him that everyone else had displayed. She demanded more than he could provide and became his most vicious opponent. Finally, she forced him to leave.

He tried to make it on his own, but he was terribly lonely. He went home and begged her to take him back. He crawled. He came back on her terms: she could take his meager salary and spend it any way she wished. She belittled his feeble attempts to support the family in front of her friends. He began to weep bitterly in the darkness of his love-deprived nightmare. He was completely and consistently without knowledge of love. But the next day he was a different person. He went to the garage and took down his rifle. He carried it with him to his newly acquired job in a book storage building. And from the third floor of that building he sent two shells crashing into the head of President John Fitzgerald Kennedy.[1]

Stories such as this rivet our attention. Love is important. Lack of love is tragedy. So we try to express love to people who are deprived of elementary things in life — food, clothing, shelter, and affection. We try to love countless refugees who have lost their homeland, many who lack financial security, and the sick who are deprived of health. Love is a solution to many people's problems.

But this is not the only kind of love 1 Corinthians 13 is talking about. Old favorite is not just talking about social improvement. Old favorite has something to say to people like us.

Ancient Corinth was a money town. But the people there really did not manufacture a great deal of goods. They were mostly collectors of money from goods others made. They were realtors, bankers, lawyers, professionals, and salesmen. They engaged primarily in trade and commerce. They were unlike the manual laborers, carpenters, farmers, builders, and fishermen that Jesus addressed in places like Nazareth, Bethlehem, and Galilee. The Corinthians were owners of ships like the fishermen Jesus addressed worked on. They handled the money from shops and furniture industries like Jesus and his father worked in as carpenters. The Corinthians were the first century's accountants, vice presidents of sales, CEO's and professors. They were also terribly good people, quite appallingly good. The Corinthians were not a bad lot at all, only a few of them. True, they did have a mountain towering above their town, topped as it was with the Temple to Aphrodite, the goddess of love. It was populated with a thousand temple prostitutes. But Corinth was the most important seaport of its day. That stuff was mostly for the out-of-towners who came during the trade seasons, kind of like the tourists who visit the red light districts in a major American city when they are far from home.

The Corinthians were affluent, church-going, and intelligent. They were new to Christianity but they were extremely wise in the ways of trade and commerce. They were competitive and totally cosmopolitan. They were like us in the fact that they were "knowledge workers." They were not laborers or small-town innkeepers and tax collectors.

Paul's letter to Corinth is an important one for us to consider. Direct production workers — bricklayers, farmers, and machinists — are a steadily declining segment of the workforce in our developed economy. They certainly are a declining segment in most churches.

The fastest growing group in our society are knowledge workers — accountants, engineers, teachers, nurses, social workers, lawyers, salesmen, and managers. People who are paid for putting knowledge to work rather than using brawn or manual skill are today the largest, and most expensive, group in America. Like the ancient Corinthians, we do interesting work, are paid well, and engage in work that does not break the body. It's nice theological meaning for us to wrestle with the parables of Jesus depicting the farmer sowing seed, the builder building on sand, and the innkeeper opening up a room for the Samaritan to house the beaten traveler. But, frankly, you and I are closer in attitude and environment to the ancient Corinthians than to the Galilean farmers, carpenters, and innkeepers.

Paul's definition of love represents a critical statement of life for us. In today's world, the motivation and satisfaction level of knowledge workers is a real problem. Today, many affluent knowledge workers are totally dissatisfied with life. Though we are paid well and have more than any generation before us, we do not know how to evaluate our lives, measure our lives, or be productive except in terms of material gain. It is taking a toll on the quality of life in our society. The alienation and lack of meaning we encounter in our world today is not primarily a phenomenon found in the working class. It is, above all, a phenomenon of the educated class of employed knowledge workers. Those are the words of Peter F. Drucker, known as "Mr. Management" in our world. He is a business professor.[2] And he's right.

At least at the end of the day the brickmason could take pride in a wall he had built; the farmer could watch the crops grow that he had planted with satisfaction, regardless of the prices they brought; the machinist could point to a piece of work turned out. Lord knows how you motivate a teacher, a preacher, a manager, a nurse, a lawyer, an accountant, and so on. Money? We've thrown money at knowledge workers. And that does motivate and provide a source of evaluation, for a while. Yet, those people get bored with their toys and houses and parties, and we all wonder if today's schoolteachers, preachers, engineers, managers, accountants, and lawyers are really more productive than their counterparts of 1900 who had even less.

Psychologist Harry Stack Sullivan maintains that *"love begins when a person feels another person's need to be as important as his own."* Frankly, life itself begins when a person feels another person's need is as important as his own. From the beginning of the Bible, the emphasis is on community. Adam is not complete without someone to love. The Lord God said, "It is not good that a man should be alone; I will make another who completes him." Adam alone is nothing; he does not even exist as a human apart from Eve. And Eve does not exist as a complete person apart from helping Adam. The helping of another person is what makes us human. Paul hammered home the point to the Corinthians: "Without love, I am nothing. Without charity I am nothing at all." Without love, regardless of my money, regardless of my power, regardless of my education, I am meaningless. Life has no meaning for me. I am dissatisfied, lonely, unfulfilled, and miserable.

To be a teacher who does not love the students, a lawyer who does not love the least of those in the community, a preacher who does not love the congregation, an accountant who does not love the unlovely, is to find no meaning in life whatsoever. Said Paul, "If I lack charity I count for nothing."

Paul was on target in broaching the subject of love with these Corinthians. They did not need a parable on evil or racism or knowledge. He was dealing with the age-old problem of the well-to-do: *Charity tends to decrease as incomes increase.* That has always been a strange fact of life. Even today it remains a truth. A Gallup Poll produced profiles of the most and least generous Americans according to income, family status, and region. It concluded that, "contrary to popular opinion, the well-to-do in America cannot be described as generous." The most likely to make contributions and volunteer their time were members of low-to-moderate income families, rural residents, and mid-Westerners.

The Bible has notions of life and death which are very different from ours today. We think of life as the functioning of the individual organism. Death is the cessation of such function. In the Bible, life means to be significantly involved in a community of caring, meaning, action, and charity. Life means relatedness. Conversely, death is to be unrelated, uncaring, and uncharitable. Death is to depart from charity. Thus to "choose life or death" (Deuteronomy 30:19) means to decide for or against the life-giving community.[3]

Paul would correctly state "If I lack charity I am nothing. In the eyes of God, I am dead. I cease to exist. I am nothing, nothing at all."

It is hard to motivate a dead person. It is hard to feel satisfied when you are religiously dead.

1 Corinthians 13. An old favorite. Yesterday's news? A sugar stick from a previous era? Perhaps not.

---

1. As told by James Dobson on a number of occasions.

2. Peter F. Drucker, *The Changing World of the Executive* (New York: Truman Talley Books, 1982), pp. 105-113.

3. Walter Brueggemann, *The Bible Makes Sense* (Atlanta: John Knox Press, 1977), pp. 109-110.

Epiphany 5

Good News For Good Living

1 Corinthians 15:1-11

The weather that Sunday was beautiful in Augusta, Georgia. The middle-aged minister and his wife, after being away eleven years, returned to their perch by the sixth tee at the Masters Golf Tournament on the Augusta National Golf Course. It was their spot. They'd sat there in former times, when they were younger, healthier, and, perhaps, less wise. Sitting beside them were two young college students. The young man was blonde and well-built. He was holding hands with a pretty coed. She was well-tanned, and had a ribbon in her long pony tail. They made a cute couple.

The minister noticed a huge ring on the right hand of the younger fellow. It was exquisite, like a World Series ring. Finally, the minister inquired about the ring. The student informed him that it was a ring given to him for playing on the conference championship football team at a certain university where he was currently a student. The young man went on to introduce the girl beside him who was a cheerleader at the same institution.

The minister's wife leaned over and whispered to him, "This is eerie. They are the same age as we were when we first met and they attend the same college from which we graduated. It's like we are sitting beside ourselves as we used to be."

The minister cleared his throat and spoke to the young man: "I used to play football at that school, too." The young man responded, "Yes, sir." The wife interjected, "And I used to be a cheerleader there." The coed looked around and said, "Yes, ma'am."

The conversation kept going and the minister winced at all the "yes sirs, no sirs, yes ma'ams, and no ma'ams." In a strange way the minister and his wife felt as if they were sitting beside their replacements in life, those who would stand in their spots after they were gone. For a brief moment amid the shouts and sounds, life was frozen by a stark revelation.

The minister forgot the golf tournament and focused for a moment in his mind on the message of the resurrection of Jesus and its claims. No longer was it fodder for a message for those who had lost loved ones so they could apply hope to their skeptical doubts. No longer was it a ready resource for counseling techniques that could bring assurances to complex biomedical decisions about when is the time to let go of a loved one.

The preponderance of the claims for the resurrection of Jesus Christ had a new-found urgency. The question was no longer, "What's going to happen to you when you die or what happened to my parents when they died?"

All it took was a chance meeting with potential replacements in life and a few "yes sirs" and "no sirs" to snap the issue around to, "What's going to happen to *me* when *I* die?"

Unfortunately during the season of Epiphany there is a tendency to view today's text as suitable only for an Easter proclamation. Yet we do well to remember that it is the "made revealed" and "recognized" nature of the resurrection faith that gives meaning to Advent, Christmas, and Epiphany.

Today's text, which reminds us of the dramatic initiative God takes in confronting us with the claims of resurrection, can become an urgent revelation for our own human condition. Just as others preceded us and remain after us in time, Paul readily acknowledges that the Easter faith preceded us and remains after us in time. In a strange way, today's text, with its loud assertion that "he was raised on the third day," can "neither be measured nor contained by time and history in any ordinary sense."[1] The Easter faith creates us; we do not create the Easter faith.

- Christ died for our sins in accordance with the Scriptures.
- He was buried.
- He was raised on the third day in accordance with the Scriptures.

- He appeared to Cephas, to the twelve, to more than five hundred people at one time, to James and all the apostles, and last of all, to Paul.

This Pauline repetition of the good news is not only one of the earliest creeds of the church, it is also our Rosetta Stone for unlocking the secrets of the human condition.

You might remember that Rosetta, now called Rashid, was a little Egyptian town, near Alexandria, at the head of the most westerly channel of the Nile Delta. During Napoleon's Egyptian expedition in 1799, a French officer discovered a piece of black marble near Rosetta. On it were words written in three languages — in Greek; in a vernacular form of Egyptian; and in hieroglyphics. For decades the Rosetta Stone meant little, if anything, to anyone. Then, in the 1820s a French archaeologist got hold of the stone. Using it as his key, he was able to read all the previously baffling hieroglyphics on monuments all over Egypt. Mysterious secrets were understood and translated through the Rosetta Stone.[2]

Today's text has been the Rosetta Stone of God for many Christians. It translates in common, everyday language some of the greatest mysteries of the universe. It is a revelation, an Epiphany, par excellence. And it speaks to all generations. Ancient Corinth is not far removed from our international world.

Essentially Corinth, a rather urbane place, was divided among five divisions of folks quite similar to those who populate our world. Gnostics believed in salvation through knowledge of God but couldn't agree with each other on their knowledge.[3] Epicureans were regarded as atheists because they believed that we "came into being out of atoms and the void ... no God had created or ruled over human beings."[4] Stoics held that the universe was a living creature animated by divine reason. Cultic people were commonly known as secular pagans. Adding to this Corinthian stew were new converts to Christianity who might have accepted baptism as a rite of passage, but may not have understood what it meant to live a Christ-like life.

Sounds all too familiar, doesn't it? People who believe but can't agree on what one must believe; those who worship objective scientific criteria as sole truth; angel worshipers who feel there is a vapor-like being animating everything in existence; thoroughly modern secularists; and those who accept but do not know how to follow Christ. We are Corinth and Corinth is us!

Paul touches all the bases. Like us, he implies that he has had no earthly contact with Jesus. Paul calls the list of those who witnessed the resurrection and asserts that "some have died." Obviously witnessing the resurrection doesn't grant immediate immortality. He notifies his charges that "last of all he appeared to me." Apparently resurrection appearances are over. The exact nature of the appearances is not Paul's concern. He is arguing for the reality of the resurrection. He is transmitting a tradition which is a summary of the proclamation of the early church:

- Christ died and was buried;
- Christ was raised and appeared.

The burial confirms a death. The appearances confirm the means by which the resurrection is perceived. In essence Paul's creed affirms two profound aspects of Jesus — his total humanity, and his intense closeness to God. These two things are bound together inextricably and are our Rosetta Stone for unlocking the mysteries of human life. We, like Christ, are human, mortal. The death rate is still one in one, in spite of every medical advancement. Our replacements are already upon the earth. As Camus says, "The human being is the only animal that knows it's going to die."

But we who are to die and be buried are, through Jesus, intensely close to God. And it is the love of this Christ that lives in the hearts of those who will one day share in his resurrection.

To reflect on Christ as risen is to reflect upon his life. The resurrection, as Paul labors to preach it, is not just a physical appearance that is the Main Event until which Jesus was just killing time with his ministry of teaching and healing. Quite the opposite. The resurrection becomes filled with meaning precisely because it is illuminated by everything Jesus had taught with his words and actions as a human being who died and was buried.

One hopes the Corinthians caught the revelation in the creed: resurrection is a matter of truly having God within each of us. Like the Corinthians of old, you and I are sometimes prone to what Bruce Bower calls "a pre-occupation with our own postmortem fate."[5]

Actually we all live in everlasting communion with a loving God who exists beyond all human knowledge and all human death.

Resurrection, then, is not about bringing people into spiritual conformity with God or anyone else. Resurrection is making people feel close to God and loved by God.

The Revelation of the "grace of God" working harder than ever through human hearts (v. 10) is the logical outcome. If a human being is a creature born to die and be raised through the love of Christ, then each human being is sacred. Humans violate God when they make a slave or a serf out of that person.

It is an epiphany, a magnificent recognition. It is this creed, not economics, science, or knowledge that predicates a free society!

Paul restates the tradition to the divided Corinthians — "This is what we preach and this is what you believed" (v. 11). It is the ultimate hope of the world. There is a new way of living in the world. It's called "good news" for "good living"!

Too often have we focused on the good news as good news for dying. Human dignity is the ever present appeal for a "good" death. A line from an old song sums up the notion: "I want to die easy when I die." Death certainly gathers in its sweep all our fears and anxieties. All of us want to die easy when we die. But is not life a vital part of that ebb and flow of existence? Is not life without dignity as crucial a blow to the human spirit as a meaningless or painful death? A good life also transcends all boundaries and horizons. As Howard Thurman states, "Life and death are identical twins."[6] A good life is made up of the same elements as a good death. The death and resurrection of Jesus redeem our living as well as our dying. That good news saves our living from the tyranny of present wants, present hungers, and present threats. The private life in its living is radically changed when the private will is infused with the will of God for God's world. The good news of Jesus is not only the Rosetta Stone that unlocks the mysteries of death. It is also the key that unlocks the deeper mysteries of how to live. Good news for good living. This is truly an Epiphany to the Gentiles in every age! So be it!

1. As quoted in Fred Craddock, John Hayes, Carl Holladay, and Gene M. Tucker, *Preaching Through the Christian Year* (Valley Forge: Trinity Press International, 1994), p. 97.

2. Robert Cleveland Holland, *Robert Holland at Shadyside* (Pittsburgh: The Shadyside Presbyterian Church, 1985), pp. 87-88.

3. George A. Buttrick, *The Interpreter's Dictionary of the Bible* (Nashville: Abingdon Press, 1962), p. 685.

4. Paul J. Achtemeier, *Harper's Bible Dictionary* (San Francisco: Harper and Row, 1985), p. 274.

5. Bruce Bower, *Stealing Jesus* (New York: Three Rivers Press, 1997), p. 45.

6. Howard Thurman, *For The Inward Journey* (Richmond, Indiana: Friends United Meeting, 1984), p. 70.

Epiphany 6

A Note To Fearful Hearts

1 Corinthians 15:12-20

The frail, tired woman had experienced a sleepless night in her hospital bed. Aged wrinkles marked her face as she prepared to greet another day of tests, medications, and well-meaning visitors. It was early. The little rays of sunshine had just begun to dance through the cracks in the window blinds.

She heard him next door. Every morning he practiced the same routine. He was a preacher. His clerical collar and oversized cross hanging from the big chain around his neck informed everyone of his status.

He wasn't her minister. Actually, he wasn't anyone's minister. But he thought he was everyone's minister. He had retired a few years earlier and his voluntary rounds in the hospital provided him with a boost to his flagging self-esteem. He would visit every patient on the hall, asking them if they "would like to have a prayer." Then, in a booming voice he would break the quiet peace of the morning hour with a recitation that would weave portions of 1 Corinthians 15 in and out of its verbiage. He always concluded, "Since Christ has risen we know that should we fall asleep we will not be lost ... Amen." Then, his duty done, the old preacher would hurry on to the next room, once again to repeat his litany.

This particular morning the frail, tired woman had had enough. Into her room he barged, ever at the ready to begin the self-selected ritual. "Would you like to have a prayer?" he intoned.

She painfully turned her head to stare him full in the face. "Sure, go ahead," she responded, "if it will make *you* feel better!"

He failed to grasp the meaning of her words and plowed ahead, reciting the prayer, and touching all the bases — "In him we will be raised ... first fruits ... those who have fallen asleep...." Then, as always, he pivoted and hurried on to the next room. She knew he would be back again the next day. His ego needed it. But she would try to make him feel as comfortable as possible.

If Christ is raised from the dead, so are we! If Christ is not raised, then neither are we. These ancient words are not meant simply as words of comfort in funeral settings. Nor are they ammunition to prop up a preacher's flagging sense of importance. They are words to address fearful hearts.

Is it all a terrible lie? Do we live under a misguided delusion? How do we see beyond the horizon of rational thought? Is this some creed from the past whose recitation is supposed to make us feel better?

Perhaps a fourth grade student said it best when she wrote to her teacher: "Laugh and the world laughs with you. Cry, and ... someone yells, 'Shut up!' " If the resurrection is not real, then all our hopes in Christ do, indeed, leave us as people to be pitied more than all people. Instead of a final victory, we will resemble little children who incessantly cry out for a parent in the middle of the dark night with a fearful heart only to hear the sharp retort thundering its way down the corridors of eternity, "Shut up and go back to sleep!"

In a world dominated by Greek reason, Paul had to argue for the actual resurrection of Jesus. The Greeks had carefully separated the body from the soul. It was a small leap for certain rationalists to argue that spirit was good and flesh was evil, both created by gods that had nothing to do with each other. Since Jesus was a part of God, then, obviously he could have never been a flesh and blood human being. How could God die? In short, there was no resurrection for there had been no death. This rational thought, filled with oriental influences and Greek mystery religions, focused on mysteries instead of realities when it came to religious expressions. Paul's focus on a bodily death and bodily resurrection must have been quite difficult for first-century converts to Christianity to understand. It was, perhaps, even more difficult for them to grasp than for us. Yet the great scandal of the resurrection of the dead remains the central belief of fearful hearts in every age, including ours.

In *Letters to a Young Poet*, Rainer Maria Rilke noted that "people have oriented all their solutions toward the easy and toward the easiest side of the easy; but it is clear that we must hold to what is difficult." When it comes to believing in the resurrection of the dead we share a common experience with the early Corinthians. We are, in our own way, new converts. In fact, in a rational and scientific world we must be converted and re-converted to this essential belief in each passing moment.

This forward-looking belief breaks the bounds of simple thought. It is anarchic in that it has not learned restraint. "Christ has been raised from the dead, the first fruits of those who have fallen asleep." This hope is a rebellious expression in our world, as well as in Paul's.

Paul's insistence that Christ died and was raised from the dead moves God from a backstage deity to a front-stage performer in human experience. God gets involved in humankind. God is fully in the human Jesus. God, then, is fully involved in all humans who die or have fallen asleep.

Paul's assertion about the resurrection is a message to fearful hearts in every age. Note that Paul is giving an answer to a question about fear — not a fear of death but a fear of performance. People in Corinth are not worried about death. They are fearful that their belief in Christ will turn out to be a fraud! The Greek world valued the opinions of others and so does our world. Essentially the issue is the same: fear of being shown up as a fraud, ignorant, a dolt! For all who are driven by a fear that someday their belief in the Christ will be exposed as inept and misguided, Paul's note is direct. The issue cannot be avoided.

If Christ has not been raised, our faith is futile. We are to be pitied. Such is the nature of faith — it is always a leap. When we believe, no explanation is necessary. When we do not believe, no explanation is satisfactory.

Christ is raised as we shall be raised — is this a great affirmation or the greatest fraud of all time? Let's be honest. On this we have wagered much. All or nothing! It demands a revolutionary response. It is a risk to believe in the resurrection.

Remember what Fred Craddock calls "The Reuben Option." Reuben is the oldest son of Jacob and is out among his brothers who are fed up with the youngest, Joseph. The brothers want to kill him. But Reuben is afraid. As the oldest, he knows that the father will most likely blame him. And, to be certain, he feels a small sense of morality in the matter. Murder is a heavy burden to bear, even if you can justify it to yourself on the basis of little Joseph's arrogant behavior. But Reuben also wants to look good in the eyes of his brothers. He takes a stand but he doesn't go far enough. Reuben tries to cover all his bases. He stands for all of us when we try to hedge, to get what we want and look good doing it. "Let's sell him," becomes Reuben's response. "Send him far away and we're rid of him." Reuben tries to keep everybody happy. He doesn't let justice get in the way of his personal ambition.

How to believe in the great affirmation but protect against the great deception? That's the formula many try to work out. To leap wholeheartedly in faith toward the resurrected Christ demands a radical lifestyle — a total involvement with humankind. You can't remain distant from the things that are contaminated in this world and those people who are sinful, like the Jewish holiness code did. You can't be apathetic like the Greek philosophers, avoiding the extremes of passion because reaching out to others always leads to disappointment. You have to understand that if the resurrection of Christ is the first fruits for a resurrection for all, then the great affirmation demands our all. We can't hedge all bets and cover our backside.

Affirmation or deception? Only our lives will tell. So be it!

Epiphany 7

The Power Of Uninformed Decisions

1 Corinthians 15:35-38, 42-50

One of the most nerve-wracking experiences in life is finding a place to live and a person to live *with*. It's as true for college students as it is for older adults. Everyone at some time or another has to house-hunt, roommate hunt, room hunt, or apartment hunt. In fact, one of the biggest changes in life occurs in college when you actually have a choice as to where you will live and with whom you will live.

The freshman experience is an *unknown* experience. You either room with someone you think you know from back home or the school assigns you a roommate. Your place to live, if you are a resident student, is given to you by the university. Someone once asked: "When you go away from home, what is the biggest adjustment you have to make?" The top four responses were: "The roommate, the roommate, the roommate, and the roommate." It's such a big decision. The same holds true when we marry another person or have children. It's an uninformed decision. There's no way to predict totally what it will be like. Even people who live together before marriage can often find that living in marriage with someone you're legally, financially, morally, and familially tied to is quite different.

Professor Stanley Hauerwas of Duke University contends that all our major decisions in life are "uninformed" decisions which require us to step out in faith. He could well be right. Consider most of our major decisions. What profession shall I enter? To whom should I be married? Should I stay married? Where should we live? When should we have children?

All of these life-changing decisions are uninformed decisions requiring a measure of trust. We certainly do not know for certain the when, where, who, and why of life until we experience it for ourselves. The critical factor in every uninformed decision would appear to be the unity and resolve with which we approach the unknown. In the base of these big questions our problem is often that we don't know the answers. All we know to do is live by faith in the God who holds all things together. That's the "good news," not the pat answer.

Today's text is a case in point. It begins with Paul having anticipated someone in the congregation in Corinth asking the questions, "How are the dead raised? With what kind of body will they come?" Even though Paul called this questioner a "fool," who hasn't been anxious about what happens after death? *Paul's problem was he didn't know.*

But Paul was the man in charge. People have always looked to the clergy and the church for answers to the big questions. The Graeco-Roman world was a world that lived to debate the issue of resurrection. The Greek idea of the immortality of the soul was the very air that the culture breathed. Paul was, in the eyes of many, the man in charge of shaping the theology of the Christian religion. By his own indirect (and often direct) admission, he was the one Christ had left in charge of the ministry to the Gentiles. He certainly was no substitute for the Christ they had lost from the world but since he was all they had, he was willing to try to answer the big questions. Like the babysitter left in charge of the children when the parents are out for the evening, Paul could never be the substitute for the Jesus who had departed this earth. Yet he was all these children in the faith had. Jesus had gone and Paul was in the pulpit and sending answers to questions being raised by the anxious children.

Like a good babysitter, Paul would not open the door to strangers and he would not let the little brothers and sisters fall down the basement steps. The children asked a question and Paul, as was his custom, wrote a quasi-official letter rather than a private letter.[1] The letter was, he hoped, one that would settle the issue and avoid the problems of opening the door of the house to strange ideas and having the children stumble.

Paul, the man in charge, knew the individuals within this multicultural congregation held several concepts of life after death. The idea of a soul separate from a body came from the Greek world. Many Greek intellectuals considered the body evil, an earthly prison for the eternal soul.[2] To Paul, this was a foreign concept which was not based on the tradition or the Scriptures he had studied as the student of Rabbi Gamaliel. Consequently he tried to argue against adopting this concept with his Greek converts lest they open the door to a strange belief. By insisting on a resurrection, Paul had closed the door to strangers.

But the children could still fall down the steps if they did not understand the universal appeal of Christ's resurrection. Burial customs in the Hellenistic and Roman periods were primarily based on the tombs of the more affluent or those who belonged to associations which provided proper burial for their members.[3] Careful not to imply that this doctrine applies only to a small group of believers out of harm's way behind locked doors, Paul began to elevate the realm of God through using his antithetical parallels: perishable/imperishable, dishonor/glory, weakness/power, and physical body/spiritual body. His final parallel leapt all the way back to creation: "The first man was of earth; the second is from heaven." Unlike Matthew who was later to track Jesus' genealogy back only to Abraham, Paul equaled the risen Christ with the redemption of the whole human race. Christ was the second Adam. Jesus was the reordering and reconstitution of all human flesh.

Paul carried his analogy of death and rebirth back to Adam to support his point. This was not the Greek idea of a soul but life as a human being, represented by the first Adam, being compared to a second Adam as a divine spirit.

By using the word "heaven" four times in the passage, Paul elevated the idea of "Savior of the World" beyond the earthly associations. This good babysitter, named Paul, did not want his children to stumble down the basement steps. Paul lived and taught under five different Roman Caesars. When Julius Caesar died in 44 B.C., the empire named him a god. He was given the title, "Savior of the World." Immediately following the death of Julius Caesar it was the practice in Rome to elevate Caesars who had died to the level of divinity as a way of honoring them. But the later Caesars, the ones contemporary with Paul and the early Christians, did not want to wait until they died to become a god. Why wait until death, since a god is a god? They insisted that they be made a god as soon as they assumed the office of Caesar. Consequently these Caesars were named gods, and citizens of the empire were supposed to worship Caesar as a god.

These Caesars were given titles that were also ascribed to Jesus, such as "Prince of Peace," and "Savior of the World."

Paul had a tough task. He had to shut the door to strange beliefs, using language people understood, yet at the same time enabling the new converts to have an understanding that Jesus was above all thrones, lest they fall down the basement steps and equate Jesus with being just another Caesar.

Paul's uninformed decision caused him to step out in faith. Jesus is not our "chum." We don't know everything about Christ — Christ goes back to creation. Christ is above any human, even Christian, attempts to explain God. The power of creation pulls all things together toward its spiritual fulfillment. Whereas the most humble material (dust) was employed to produce the first humanity; the second creation had its origin from heaven and brought a new nature to humanity.[4]

What a babysitter. Paul explained in understandable terms his concept of the resurrection of the body as a plan of God. Christ was first but Christ was a prototype for all in the final victory of God.[5]

You and I do not know all there is to know about life and death. We are uninformed. Paul's method remains applicable to us. Jesus is gone and we are here. But take heart: where Christ is, we shall also be. Our job in the interim is to keep from opening the door to strange New Age beliefs and avoid falling down the steps into worshiping any earthly person or group. There is a power available to us in this greatest of all uninformed decisions. It's called faith.

---

1. Bruce Metzger, ed., *The New Oxford Annotated Bible* (New York: Oxford University Press, 1991). The letters attributed to Paul were much longer than

other ancient letters. The average private letter on papyrus contained 87 words, whereas Paul's letters averaged about 1300 words.

2. Graydon F. Snyder, *First Corinthians: A Faith Community Commentary* (Macon, Georgia: Mercer University Press, 1992), p. 253.

3. Victor H. Matthews, *Manners and Customs in the Bible* (Boston: Hendrickson Publishers, 1991), p. 239.

4. See William F. Orr and James A. Walther, *The Anchor Bible* (Garden City, New York: Doubleday, 1976).

5. James M. Efird, *How to Interpret the Bible* (Atlanta: John Knox Press, 1984), p. 118.

Epiphany 8

Taking The Sting Out Of Death

1 Corinthians 15:51-58

One of the most lasting images in the New Testament is one from Saint Paul: O death, where is thy victory? O death, where is thy sting?

The early Christians asserted that Jesus has taken the sting out of death by demonstrating that it is but a doorway into another realm.

Have you ever been badly stung? If so, you will recognize the importance of removing the pain and being surrounded by a group of fellow laborers, just like the Bible says.

A minister relates the earliest memory from his childhood when he was four years old. His father owned a little hardware store in a small town. The father employed a handyman named Buster. Old Buster could do just about anything and would in order to earn a living. On Sunday afternoons when the store was closed, Buster would take care of the lawn and shrubbery at the owner's house. One Sunday, Buster's assigned task was to saw off the dead limb from a huge bush by the side porch. It was a dreadfully hot day and the owner's child was barefooted and without a shirt. No one else was in the yard, just old Buster and the child. The little boy was slurping on a popsicle and Buster was sawing the limb. Now, Buster and the boy used to talk a lot. They were talking when the limb finally cracked off. As that limb cracked, another sound filled the air. It sounded like a huge buzz. Buster screamed, turned around and ran right over the child. The hornets stung the boy all over his face and upper body. The boy even later in his adult years vividly remembered what happened next: he never did cry. As soon as Buster screamed, the whole neighborhood was mobilized. His mother had him in her arms and was rubbing butter and ointment over the stings. Neighbors came dashing over with ice, and the physician from next door, who was cutting his grass, came over in a flash. Actually it was comforting to have the sting removed and to be surrounded by so many friends.

The second time that same child was stung things were quite different. It was twenty years later and he had become "citified." He had lived in Boston for three years in a dormitory in an area with 30,000 people per square mile. That summer he accepted a job in a large church back in his home state as a youth director. His first week in town he dreamed up what he thought was a good project. Many years previously the church had erected a welcome sign at each of the six main highways leading into the city. Underneath the welcome were printed the address of the church and the hour of worship. But time and weather had taken their toll on the signs. The paint was peeling off and the general appearance had deteriorated. It was an obvious project — to repaint the signs. So one Saturday morning he set out to scrape the flaking paint with wire brushes. The first sign was overrun with bushes. He went in with a little axe and started hacking away. Very soon afterwards, he heard and saw what he and old Buster had heard and seen many years earlier. Those hornets really stung him.

He wrapped up his hands and face in paper towels and drove as fast as he could to a physician's office. The doctor was at the beach for the weekend, but the secretaries directed him to a clinic where he could be seen. When he arrived at the clinic there were at least thirty people in the huge waiting room. He did not know a soul. His name got at the bottom of the list. For an hour and twenty minutes he sat there by himself among strangers. Then a nurse took his name to the back. Two doctors came rushing out. When they found he had been there that long, they said, "Go on home. If you had been allergic you would have passed out by now."

It really makes a difference when the sting isn't taken out and you can't see the familiar faces of friends and coworkers.

The Apostle Paul states that "the last enemy to be destroyed is death" (1 Corinthians 15:26). Death is the ultimate sting. It is the final meeting toward which our lives move. Saint Augustine says in one of his sermons, as a physician leans over the cot of a sick man and pronounces gravely, "He will die, he shall not get over this," so one might look into a crib on the first day of a baby's life and say, "She will die, she will not get over this."[1]

Life is terminal. There is a sting to it. Everyday — despite the growing of the grass, the chatter of the animals, the ecstasies of the moment, the plaques on the wall in our den, and the eternal movement of the universe — is a step closer to this final sting. As Will Willimon says, "Whoever doesn't know this knows nothing."[2]

One of the deepest problems in our day is perhaps the reality that our society has put the sting back in death. There have been healthier times when society did not go to such great lengths to keep death out of sight and out of mind. The sting of death was not as great because it was an experience lived with each day. The burial ground surrounded the church which itself stood in the center of the community. It was impossible to avoid the cemetery, the church, and the importance of the friends and coworkers gone before us. Moreover, a person was buried from the church, the same place where that person was baptized and married and sat with the children and friends on Sunday mornings. Today we hide our burial grounds and sometimes even our churches on the outskirts of town where we rarely have to see them. And the complexities of our schedules often mean we want to be associated with a good church but not deeply involved in one. Sometimes it appears that the sting is back and the cloud of witnesses is gone.

Wouldn't it be life-changing if we could have the sting of death removed and begin to see life as a victorious enterprise? Nothing would have greater impact on our daily lives than having our negative feelings about death removed — to learn again that we have been mistaken in our fears.

Paul wrote the Corinthians that there is no sting in death for those who know Christ. They could sing and live in great joy because their eyes produced a brief but real "double exposure" so that right behind the wall of terror they could see the one who received them. The sting was removed from death for them because Jesus had demonstrated that it is but a doorway into another realm just as our birth from our mother's womb was but a doorway into this world.

In a prenatal state a baby is happy in its mother's womb. Tucked up under its mother's heart, it is already sensitive to love. Suppose we could get across to such an unborn fetus the realization, "You can't stay here forever. You're going to be born." That to the baby would be death. It would mean a change from security to insecurity, from a certainty to an uncertainty. You can imagine the thinking of the infant. "I want to stay here. I'm comfortable. I'm fed. I'm loved."

When a baby is born, that infant is screaming and shaking all over. The infant shakes in fear with every fiber of its being. Going into a new world is frightening.

But as the child grows and feels accepted by the mother around the child, it begins to love life and to love this world. Time passes. And he becomes middle-aged. And perhaps, an old man. The thought comes to him, "I want to stay here. I'm fed. I'm loved. I don't want to go from certainty to uncertainty, from security to insecurity."

But this time, asserts the Christian, there is a difference. Someone outside this womb of our existence has actually come into the world with us, died, gone beyond it, and given us a glimpse of the final birth. There is no greater light breaking into the stream of human existence than that moment when Mary Magdalene runs to the disciples and exclaims, "I have seen the Lord. I have seen the Lord. He is risen. He is risen." Like the soft roll of a kettledrum announcing something important over the enveloped shades of fear, she walks toward her destiny. The violins and horns tune up and, finally, the full orchestration of the gospel hits the world like a triumphant climax heralding the start of a new day — "I have seen the Lord. He is risen. There is no sting. I have seen over to the other side." There is no sting in death, is the way Paul put things to his new charges in ancient Corinth.

Like a prairie fire flying from heart to heart, that message captured humankind. Up against the mighty empires came these simple Christian people saying that in the name of Jesus people could live. They were witnesses to it. They were the first cloud of witnesses to those who live on earth that the sting is removed, the last enemy destroyed, the greatest obstacle to a happy life removed. Generation flows into generation. We can live with a quiet and simple confidence in the continuation of life after death. "Let nothing move you. Always give yourself fully to the work of the Lord, because you know that your labor in the Lord is not in vain" (v. 58). This assertion is so grand that we can cease the common practice of avoidance. Most of the time we are so involved in life that we would like to postpone as long as we can any consideration that ultimately every journey that has a beginning has an ending, a final destination.

She was in her mid-eighties. The pain was fresh and raw. Her malignancy was advanced. Her son called her on the phone. "Are you afraid?" he asked. "No," she said. "My mother went like this; my brother went like this; hundreds of thousands of people go like this each year. If they can do it, I guess I can." Sensing his fear, she said, "It's all right. I have more people over there waiting to say hello to me than I have here to say goodbye to."[3]

And that is precisely what you and I shall have, kin and friends living in a home, waiting for our arrival. As we quickly reach a point in life where we realize that the earth will go on without us, death can, indeed, begin to lose much of its sting.

---

1. See William H. Willimon, "The Last Enemy," *The Christian Century* (March 21-28, 1984), p. 293.

2. *Ibid.*

3. Quoted by James Armstrong, Bishop of the United Methodist Church, Dakotas Areas, in a sermon, "An Endless Tryst."

*Transfiguration Of Our Lord
(Last Sunday After The Epiphany)*

Exposed!

2 Corinthians 3:12—4:2

Today is the end of the season of Epiphany, which began the first Sunday in January. Throughout the Advent, Christmas, and Epiphany seasons we have been celebrating ways in which God's glory has been manifested in the life of Jesus. If these ways were easy to understand by early Christians, Paul would not have had to write all those letters.

This is Transfiguration Sunday and, once again, we are presented with another experience in the life of Jesus that appears to be outside our frame of reference.

One of the amazing stories in the New Testament is that account of the Transfiguration. Jesus took Peter, James, and John with him and led them up a high mountain. His clothes became dazzling white, whiter than anyone in the world could bleach them. And there appeared Elijah and Moses, the two great former teachers, who were talking with Jesus.

Peter got real excited over this mountaintop experience. "Rabbi," he said, "this is wonderful. It's so good to be here. Let's hold on to this forever. Let's put up three shelters, three monuments, one for you, one for Moses, and one for Elijah" (Mark 9:2-6).

It was quite a scene and Peter wanted to make it permanent. Three permanent shelters with Jesus, Moses, and Elijah in them; what a tourist attraction that would be! Hundreds of thousands of people would make a pilgrimage to that place. Yet Jesus said, "Let it go. We cannot live on the mountaintop." The disciples looked around and they no longer saw anyone with them except Jesus. They had to come down the mountain and return to the reality of suffering and pain. As they came down the mountain they found a large crowd arguing with the teachers of the law. Next they encountered a boy with some kind of epileptic seizure.

What a strange person this Jesus appeared to be. His life was all wrapped up in mystery and holy times. But he told his disciples not to hold on to any of them. Peter, James, and John could not freeze the mountaintop experience.

Jesus apparently knew that *a life only of inspiring moments and sacred knowledge limits the God who will be who God will be in the ordinary experiences of life.*

For the early Christians, the life of Jesus was often seen through the life of Moses. Certainly a religious leader had to look like a religious leader and act like a religious leader was supposed to act in order to be accepted. In the epistle lesson for this morning, Paul utilizes the Old Testament story about the veil of Moses as an analogy to talk about the Christian life. The tie between the epistle lesson and the Transfiguration is an appropriate one. Moses, Elijah, and Jesus were the three great professors of the Judeo-Christian heritage. Moses, the lawgiver, Elijah, the founder of the first seminary, and Jesus, who is called "Rabbi" by Peter in the mountaintop experience, represent the totality of the legal, prophetic, and evangelical perspectives.

Paul harkens the religious memory back to the Old Testament scene where Moses comes down from Mount Sinai with the tablets of stone on which are chiseled the Ten Commandments. The people are focusing not on the tablets but on the face of Moses. They can see that something had happened to Moses up on the mountain. Moses' appearance has been shaped by his experience with God. It was in his face. Consequently Moses wears a veil over his face because people were afraid to look there. The Old Testament Jew is forbidden to look into the brightness of God. One had to be veiled from the glory of God.

Paul's message to the Corinthians clearly states that the Christian experience is to be the exact opposite of people's response to Moses. Just as the Hebrews looked at Moses and knew he had been talking with God, so people should be able to see in the face of Christians some evidence that they have been with Jesus. In short, Christians have an unveiled face when it comes to letting the world behold the glory of God. The love of Christ will shine through the faces of those who have encountered Jesus and through the institution called church which houses these shining Christians. Unfortunately that has not always been the case with either Christians or their churches. Many of our doctrines have become veils which systematize the faith and hide the love of God behind tinted windows and closed blinds. In fact, a psychiatrist once described modern day Christians as being like hypochondriac widows living behind closed blinds or tinted windows, holding to memories of a dead husband. Christianity can, indeed, become a veiled experience, separating us from our fellow human beings as we retreat into what Paul calls "secret and shameful ways" (4:2).

Paul clearly renounces the "chosen people" ideal of legalistically keeping to laws (the Jews had 613 of them) as a kind of divine insurance policy. Rather than viewing faith in Christ as a divine aspirin to take in secret to ease morbid anxieties over our own health, Paul is encouraging his charges to expose themselves and let their faith become public as it interacts with the world around them. In this regard, Paul's mysticism shines through. He sees the love of Christ as a power pulling all things together toward their fulfillment. As others see the radiance in the loving lives of Christians, true freedom is experienced for those who see Christ in us.

Can you and I remain Christian in an affluent society if all we do is sit behind tinted windows and closed blinds, wondering about our own health and personal salvation? This sermon probably doesn't feel very comfortable, for you or for me. But, in the final analysis, I'm not certain how much God cares about our feelings. God appears to be as much concerned about the way we treat others in our world and the visions we exchange with one another as God does the way we feel about ourselves. God apparently wants us to expose ourselves to the public.

Paul's insistence that this reflection of the Lord's glory is an ever-increasing event cautions against an episodic approach to this exposure. We have a ministry that is to reflect the ministry of the Lord himself. That ministry of Jesus was very much a public ministry in which he called on those who followed him to visit the prisoners, feed the hungry, heal the sick, clothe the naked, and welcome the stranger.

On the sidewalks by the Tower of London, a man was busily sketching pictures in chalk. Near him sat his ragged hat into which people would throw coins if they admired his efforts to paint the sidewalks. All day long this artist worked on his pictures. Some were beautiful scenes of the countryside while others were of fruit and flowers that appeared to passersby to be sitting on the sidewalks. A passing shower would work havoc with the drawings. Someone would occasionally walk over one by mistake. The artist was forever retouching the drawings.[1]

Destroyed every night, the pictures were redrawn each morning, always by the same artist. Despite the polite form of begging, many wished the artist had used a more permanent form for his beautiful expressions.

The world is full of people who paint masterpieces in chalk — people who exhaust all their energies on enterprises which seldom last longer than a night.

You and I are the exposed, permanent materials which God uses to paint to the world Jesus' vision of the Kingdom of God coming on earth as it will in heaven. This is why Paul uses such terms as "freedom," "ministry," "renounced secret and shameful ways."

In a country like ours where the disparity between rich and poor is growing and every 44 minutes an American child dies of the effects of poverty, a veiled faith will not work. We must do more than form clubs to discuss hunger. We must do more than debate the morality of the appearance of those who are naked. We must do more than offer the sick our private prayers thanking God for our own health.

If Christ truly be within us, the veil has been lifted from our personage. We are exposed!

---

1. This example is given by Roy L. Simth, "Masterpieces in Chalk," *Sidewalk Sermons,* Abingdon Press, pp. 39-40.

Books In This Cycle C Series

GOSPEL SET

Praying For A Whole New World
Sermons For Advent/Christmas/Epiphany
William G. Carter

Living Vertically
Sermons For Lent/Easter
John N. Brittain

Changing A Paradigm — Or Two
Sermons For Sundays After Pentecost (First Third)
Glenn E. Ludwig

Topsy-Turvy: Living In The Biblical World
Sermons For Sundays After Pentecost (Middle Third)
Thomas A. Renquist

Ten Hits, One Run, Nine Errors
Sermons For Sundays After Pentecost (Last Third)
John E. Berger

FIRST LESSON SET

The Presence In The Promise
Sermons For Advent/Christmas/Epiphany
Harry N. Huxhold

Deformed, Disfigured, And Despised
Sermons For Lent/Easter
Carlyle Fielding Stewart III

Two Kings And Three Prophets For Less Than A Quarter
Sermons For Sundays After Pentecost (First Third)
Robert Leslie Holmes

What If What They Say Is True?
Sermons For Sundays After Pentecost (Middle Third)
John W. Wurster

A Word That Sets Free
Sermons For Sundays After Pentecost (Last Third)
Mark Ellingsen

SECOND LESSON SET
You Have Mail From God!
Sermons For Advent/Christmas/Epiphany
Harold C. Warlick, Jr.

Hope For The Weary Heart
Sermons For Lent/Easter
Henry F. Woodruff

A Hope That Does Not Disappoint
Sermons For Sundays After Pentecost (First Third)
Billy D. Strayhorn

Big Lessons From Little-Known Letters
Sermons For Sundays After Pentecost (Middle Third)
Kirk W. Webster

Don't Forget This!
Robert R. Kopp
Sermons For Sundays After Pentecost (Last Third)

www.ingramcontent.com/pod-product-compliance
Lightning Source LLC
Chambersburg PA
CBHW071722040426
42446CB00011B/2171